pray

a word a day

— VOLUME 2 —

pray
a word a day
— VOLUME 2 —

Connecting to God One Word at a Time

editors of guideposts

Pray a Word a Day volume 2
Published by Guideposts Books & Inspirational Media
100 Reserve Road, Suite E200, Danbury, CT 06810
Guideposts.org

Acknowledgments

Every attempt has been made to credit the sources of copyrighted material used in this book. If any such acknowledgment has been inadvertently omitted or miscredited, receipt of such information would be appreciated.

Scripture quotations marked (AMP) are taken from the *Amplified Bible*. Copyright © 2015 by The Lockman Foundation, La Habra, California. All rights reserved.

Scripture quotations marked (CEB) are taken from the *Common English Bible*. Copyright © 2011 by Common English Bible.

Scripture quotations marked (CSB) are taken from *The Christian Standard Bible*, copyright © 2017 by Holman Bible Publishers. Used by permission.

Scripture quotations marked (ERV) are taken from *Easy-to-Read Version Bible*, copyright © 2006 by Bible League International.

Scripture quotations marked (ESV) are taken from the *Holy Bible, English Standard Version*. Copyright © 2001 by Crossway Bibles, a division of Good News Publishers. Used by permission. All rights reserved.

Scripture quotations marked (GNT) are taken from the *Holy Bible, Good News Translation*. Copyright © 1992 by American Bible Society.

Scripture quotations marked (HCSB) are taken from the *Holman Christian Standard Bible*. Copyright © 1999, 2000, 2002, 2003, 2009 by Holman Bible Publishers, Nashville, Tennessee. All rights reserved.

Scripture quotations marked (JPS) are taken from *Tanakh: A New Translation of the Holy Scriptures according to the Traditional Hebrew Text*. Copyright © 1985 by the Jewish Publication Society. All rights reserved.

Scripture quotations marked (KJV) are taken from the *King James Version of the Bible*.

Scripture quotations marked (MSG) are taken from *The Message*. Copyright © 1993, 1994, 1995, 1996, 2000, 2001, 2002 by Eugene H. Peterson.

Scripture quotations marked (NABRE) are taken from the *New American Bible*, revised edition, © 2010, 1991, 1986, 1970 Confraternity of Christian Doctrine, Inc., Washington, DC. All Rights Reserved.

Scripture quotations marked (NASB) are taken from the New American Standard Bible®, Copyright © 1960, 1971, 1977, 1995, 2020 by The Lockman Foundation. All rights reserved.

Scripture quotations marked (NCV) are taken from *The Holy Bible, New Century Version*. Copyright © 2005 by Thomas Nelson.

Scripture quotations marked (NIV) are taken from *The Holy Bible, New International Version*. Copyright © 1973, 1978, 1984, 2011 by Biblica, Inc. Used by permission of Zondervan. All rights reserved worldwide. zondervan.com

Scripture quotations marked (NKJV) are taken from *The Holy Bible, New King James Version*. Copyright © 1982 by Thomas Nelson.

Scripture quotations marked (NLT) are taken from the *Holy Bible, New Living Translation*. Copyright © 1996, 2004, 2007 by Tyndale House Foundation. Used by permission of Tyndale House Publishers Inc., Carol Stream, Illinois. All rights reserved.

Scripture quotations marked (NLV) are from the *New Life Bible*, copyright © 1969 by Christian Literature International. Used by permission. All rights reserved.

Scripture quotations marked (NRSVUE) are taken from the *New Revised Standard Version, Updated Edition*. Copyright © 2021 National Council of Churches of Christ in the United States of America. Used by permission. All rights reserved worldwide.

Scripture quotations marked (PHILLIPS) are taken from *The New Testament in Modern English by J.B Phillips* copyright © 1960, 1972 J. B. Phillips. Administered by The Archbishops' Council of the Church of England. Used by Permission.

Scripture quotations marked (RSV) are taken from the *Revised Standard Version of the Bible*. Copyright © 1946, 1952, 1971 by the Division of Christian Education of the National Council of the Churches of Christ in the United States of America. Used by permission.

Scripture quotations marked (TLB) are taken from *The Living Bible*. Copyright © 1971 by Tyndale House Publishers, Inc., Carol Stream, Illinois. All rights reserved.

Scripture quotations marked (VOICE) are taken from *The Voice Bible*. Copyright 2012 Thomas Nelson, Inc. The Voice™ translation copyright © 2012 Ecclesia Bible Society. All rights reserved.

Scripture quotations marked (WEB) are taken from the *World English Bible*, which is in the public domain.

Cover and interior design by Serena Fox, Bean Inc.
Cover photo by Shutterstock
Typeset by Aptara, Inc.

ISBN 978-1-961125-77-3 (hardcover)
ISBN 978-1-961125-78-0 (softcover)
ISBN 978-1-961125-76-6 (epub)

Printed and bound in the United States of America

The word is very near you; it is in your mouth
and in your heart so you may obey it.

—*Deuteronomy 30:14 (NIV)*

Introduction

A single word can change your day. Your life, even.

My girlfriend and I had been dating for nearly two years. She'd been my dream girl, my "uber woman," long before, when we were simply friends, and there was no doubt in my mind that I wanted to spend my life with her—if she'd have me. So it was a welcome surprise when she started talking about our future in terms that suggested we'd someday get married. We discussed the usual topics—how many children we might have, what education and career plans we might pursue, and so on. But one day, when the topic of possible wedding plans came up again, quite casually, in the kitchen of her parents' apartment, she further surprised me.

"You know, you never asked me to marry you."

I had no ring to give her. I had made no plans for a proposal. But there and then, I dropped to one knee in front of the refrigerator, took her hand in mine, and asked her to marry me.

Far from the most romantic proposal of all time, but she said yes.

One word. One syllable, in fact. But it held a world—a universe—of meaning and blessing for me. It amazed me. Overwhelmed me. And set the trajectory of the rest of my life.

A single word can say and do so much. When a sign appears on a footpath, saying, "Danger." When a child utters a first word: "Mommy" or "Daddy." When a lab report conveys the news: "Benign."

The power of one simple word becomes still greater when it becomes a prayer. I don't recall exactly when I started praying one-word prayers, but I've been doing so for many years now. It probably started as "Lord, have mercy," or "Come, Lord Jesus," during a time of particular (and perhaps painful) need in my life. Soon, however, my pursuit of unceasing prayer throughout the day (see 1 Thessalonians 5:17) prompted a frequent focus on just one word at a time: "Help," sometimes, or "Bless," or "Come." I would repeat the word frequently throughout the day, and found the practice to be helpful, comforting, focusing, and, at times, tremendously illuminating.

At some point after I started blogging on the subject of prayer for the Guideposts website, I suggested a one-word prayer for specific situations. That post, and subsequent "one-word prayer" pieces I wrote, engendered so many likes, comments, and shares, I was encouraged to say more on the subject. These articles eventually led the insightful folks at Guideposts to conceive a book titled *Pray a Word a Day*, to which I was honored to contribute. That undated, 365-day devotional focused on a single word in each reading, inspiring readers to be intentional about connecting with God by focusing on and praying that word throughout each day. The reception that book enjoyed has led to the volume you hold in your hands.

Like its predecessor, *Pray a Word a Day* volume 2 invites you to journey through a year's worth of daily readings that will inspire, comfort, delight, and challenge you with a daily word to pray and meditate on. Each day's entry starts with an inspirational quote or Bible verse centered on a simple, common word. A short true story from one of the many contributing writers will follow, ending with a prayer designed to help you turn to God and invite Him to speak and act in your life. As you carry the word of the day with you and reflect on it through your day, you may be surprised at how God shows up in your life, perhaps using that word as a nudge or a tap on your shoulder. You may encounter that word in an email or television commercial. You may notice it on a billboard or in conversation with a friend.

God may use such moments to remind you that He is present, watching and speaking to your heart.

Because this book's selections are undated, you can start anytime, absorbing a veritable feast of 365 meditations and using each day's focus to inspire and direct your prayers. Each day's short entry takes mere minutes to read, and at the bottom of each page you'll find space to jot down your heart's response, if you so choose. You may even want to share copies of this book with others—family members, friends, and neighbors—who might unite in prayer by focusing on the same word every day with you and with one another.

So, welcome to *Pray a Word a Day 2*. May God use it to help you experience the joy, freedom, and purpose of prayer in your daily life . . . one word at a time.

Faithfully yours,
Bob Hostetler

bow

. . . in reverence I bow down . . . —Psalm 5:7 (NIV)

A square dance begins with the call to honor your partner, which is done with a bow. A bow is how you begin. I aim to practice this in my daily life. Begin with a bow. Approach with reverence and honor that which awaits me. When I do, I find it de-escalates both me and whomever or whatever I am about to engage, be it people, projects, or even my chronic pain. Approaching with a grumble or a growl only results in a tangled mess, with me tripping over the other person or situation instead of enjoying the dance.

What might change if I were to take one quick moment of reverent pause before engaging with what or who is before me? In deference and preference, why not bow? In honor and humility, in respect and reverence, let us bow to begin.

Honor one another. Honor your Partner. Bow to begin.

—Jenny Gehman

God, help me today to begin with a bow. Amen.

start

He will drink from a brook along the way, and so
he will lift his head high. —Psalm 110:7 (NIV)

I woke, craving a drink of water, my throat dry and head pounding. I had filled a thirty-two-ounce glass the night before, and now I downed it in two long gulps. Then I began my day, showering, dressing, and completing all the necessary tasks before my workday.

When I sat down to eat breakfast, I realized my headache was gone. At the start of the new day, my body made it very clear what it needed. Water.

The thought came to me: *How often do I listen to my soul's need for refreshing? How often do I rush to get my body ready for work without preparing my heart for the day?*

I set my spoon down and opened my Bible. As I filled my stomach with oatmeal, I nourished my mind and soul with God's Word. The right start for every day.

—Beth Gormong

Lord, help me start my days nourishing my soul the way I satisfy my body after a long night without water and food.

plant

You will bring them in and plant them on the mountain of
your inheritance—the place, LORD, you made for your
dwelling, the sanctuary, LORD, your hands established.
—Exodus 15:17 (NIV)

When my husband, Craig, finished his Army obligation, the road trip from Kansas to our forever home in the Sierra Valley was challenging. He drove a U-Haul truck and pulled one car while I drove his large flatbed truck and pulled another. Each of us had a baby in tow too—he, our twenty-one-month-old, and I, our seven-month-old. Those were pre-GPS, pre-cell phone days, so relief settled in when we reached our mountain valley for the first time. And I prayed.

Lord, if you will plant me here, I will dedicate our home to your service. It will be a sanctuary for whoever needs a place to stay.

The following four decades served as a garden for exchange students, countless ministry gatherings, foster children, and young adults in transition. God truly planted us in our small, rural community, and our life here has caused us to blossom.

—Janet Holm McHenry

Lord, plant me purposefully in my community
for the sake of serving others and You.

soar

Those who hope in the LORD will renew their strength. They will soar on wings like eagles; they will run and not grow weary, they will walk and not be faint. —Isaiah 40:31 (NIV)

I love high vistas—mountaintops, skyscrapers, airplanes. They offer some of the best views, and they infuse my spirit with a feeling of freedom. Eagles represent that same sense of freedom to me. They fly high above the earth and don't fear a storm. When they face turbulent winds, they do not seek shelter like other birds, but use the force of the updrafts to rise higher and higher. They "lock" their wings and glide effortlessly above it without using their own energy.

We, too, can "lock" our trust on God when we face life's storms. The Bible promises us that if we put our hope in God, He will renew our strength and cause us to "soar" on wings like eagles, to run and not grow weary, to walk and not faint.

—Sandra Kay Chambers

Lord, when I face storms in my life, help me to "lock"
my faith on You so I can soar above them like the eagle.

bond

Be completely humble and gentle; be patient, bearing with one another in love. Make every effort to keep the unity of the Spirit through the bond of peace. —Ephesians 4:2–3 (NIV)

B onding is a vital element for many things to work properly. Whether it's affixing two surfaces or bonding human hearts, both need to be joined to work together in harmony.

It's interesting that heat or pressure is often used as a binding agent for adhesives. Isn't that like personal relationships? Often when we face fiery trials or life's pressures with others, it creates bonds. We hear of this all the time with war comrades and police officers.

Paul urges us to strive for that goal among fellow believers. Without the same connection to our brothers and sisters in Christ, we cannot please the Lord. Maintaining peace and love with one another is what binds us, nurtures true fellowship, and models Christ's love to the watching world.

—Tez Brooks

Lord, forgive me if I have neglected or avoided godly fellowship. Help me bond closely to my spiritual family. Amen.

knit

For it was you who formed my inward parts; you knit me together in my mother's womb. —Psalm 139:13 (NRSVUE)

A country store hereabouts sells knitted items—mittens, socks, stocking caps—made from locally produced wool. In a side room, you can watch as three women operate foot-pedal spinning wheels, turning clouds of wool into yarn in a process as old as the Bible. You can smell the lanolin. On the wall behind the women there hangs a wooden sign: I Knit, Therefore I Am.

To knit is to make a garment, but in a broader sense the verb means to unite, to interlock, to mend. My one-word prayer for today is: *knit*. For fractured family relationships, O Lord: knit. For the churches in my community, too long separated into competitive camps, O Lord: knit. For the disparate impulses and motives of my life, pulling me this way and that, instead of uniting in a desire to seek first the Kingdom of God, O Lord: knit.

—Lou Lotz

God of grace, who knit me together in my mother's womb, knit my thoughts, words, and deeds into a single passion to live for You. Amen.

hair

And even the very hairs of your head are all numbered.
—Matthew 10:30 (NIV)

Hot water cascaded down on my head. If only it could wash away the worries swirling in my mind. Grabbing the shampoo bottle, I poured the thick, white liquid onto my palm and applied it to my hair.

After rinsing the cleaner off, I opened my eyes and happened to notice strands of hair strewn on the shower floor. *Great. Now I'll have to clean up what I'd shed.* All I saw was another item for my already lengthy to-do list.

Later, kneeling to remove the hair, my perspective changed. While I saw a mess to clean up, I realized that God saw how many hairs had fallen. He knows me intimately, down to the number of hairs on my head. If He knows that fact, He knows my concerns and desires, and He knows how to guide me as I face them. Why pull my hair out with worry when He is there for me?

—Alice H. Murray

Dear God: No one knows me better and cares for me more than You. I am blessed that nothing about me, even the number of hairs on my head, escapes Your notice and concern. Amen.

taste

Taste and see that the LORD is good; blessed is the one who takes refuge in him. —Psalm 34:8 (NIV)

S ugar is my love language. To taste it is to love it. For most of my life, it was a close companion that stood ready to soothe, comfort, and lift my spirits at a moment's notice. Just the sound of an ice-cream container lid peeling away from the half-gallon carton turned me into a giddy ten-year-old.

But a prediabetic scare called for changes to my diet. And I made many, swapping unhealthy sweets for better options. My favorite food swap is adding blueberries instead of brown sugar to my oatmeal. Unlike brown sugar, blueberries are unpredictable: sometimes tart, sometimes sweet. It's not until I bite and taste the berries for myself that I experience how sweet they can be.

In the same way, someone who's only heard about the Lord's goodness might think it's unpredictable, like the blueberries. It's not until we taste it for ourselves, through a growing relationship with Jesus, that we savor the brown-sugar sweetness of His faithfulness and provision.

—Cathy Baker

Lord, like David, I desire to draw near to You, to taste Your goodness, and to tell others what You have done for me. Amen.

remodel

I will give them an undivided heart and put a new spirit in them; I will remove from them their heart of stone and give them a heart of flesh. —Ezekiel 11:19 (NIV)

We've done our share of projects around our house. We've lived in the same place for twenty-two years, so there isn't a room we haven't touched. Our most recent large project was our kitchen. We ripped out all our old cabinetry; put in clean, white Ikea cabinets; created a coffee corner; and added a nice stone backsplash under the cabinets over the stove. It looks really great. It was a messy process. We made some mistakes. There was a lot of dust along the way. But the process was worth it.

God, the Master Builder, wants to renovate our hearts. Where things have grown old, He wants to revive them. Where corners have been cut, He wants to rebuild even stronger. His reno jobs always make us better. The question is, will we let Him into every part of our hearts?

—Stephanie Reeves

God, remake my heart of stone into a heart of flesh,
one that looks more like Jesus. Amen.

carousel

Rejoice in the Lord always. I will say it again: Rejoice!
—Philippians 4:4 (NIV)

The pride of my small town is its historic carousel. Lions, unicorns, quail, and frogs race alongside the brightly colored horses. Mirrors and music reflect light and joy as riders young and old circle past.

Life is like a merry-go-round, filled with ups and downs. On this course that sometimes seems to lead us in circles, there's still so much to be grateful for. When I slow down after a whirlwind ride, I see the changes Jesus has created within me and throughout my world. Looking at the others on this ride of faith, I see the uniqueness He's blessed each of us with—like the colorful mounts that carry their riders around—and I rejoice. I know where I've come from and where I'm going. He's riding at my side on life's carousel.

—Heidi Gaul

Lord, bless me with Your light and joy as I ride life's ups and downs today. Amen.

vessel

Therefore, if anyone cleanses himself from the latter,
he will be a vessel for honor, sanctified and useful for
the Master, prepared for every good work.
—2 Timothy 2:21 (NKJV)

I have many vessels in my kitchen. My bowls and pitchers come in all sizes, shapes, and colors. But I don't use my vessels to *do* something, like my spatulas and whisks—rather, they are meant to *contain* something. When I fill them, they can serve many purposes.

God's Word tells us that we are vessels for Him. He desires to fill us with Himself. While we can *do* many things to serve Him, we can also serve simply by being containers for His honor and glory and mercy. The world wants to fill us with wealth, fame, and power. But God wants to fill us with His Spirit so He can use us for His kingdom.

Our vessels might leak or even tip over and empty with the challenges of daily living. But when we keep our hearts thirsty for the Spirit, God will provide fresh blessings to fill it.

—Becky Van Vleet

O God, use me and fill me with Your almighty love
so that I may be a vessel for You.

blemish

The LORD does not look at the things people look at. People look at the outward appearance, but the LORD looks at the heart. —1 Samuel 16:7 (NIV)

The doctor said the scar on my forehead was healing nicely, but I thought the red crease where he removed a cancerous spot was ugly and embarrassing. At first I covered it with a bandage when out in public, but at home, I removed the uncomfortable strip.

On my way to meet a friend for lunch one day, I looked in the mirror and realized I had forgotten to cover the scar. No doubt she would notice and ask about it.

When she arrived at the restaurant, we became engrossed in conversation, and I forgot about my scar. But then I noticed she also had a red crease in her forehead. Was it an injury, a scar, or just a wrinkle? She didn't say a word about my scar, so I didn't ask about hers. In that moment, I realized that while neither of us looked perfect, the friendship we enjoyed was more important.

—Marilyn Turk

Lord, thank You for loving me despite my imperfections.

till

Sow righteousness for yourselves, reap the fruit of unfailing love, and break up your unplowed ground; for it is time to seek the Lord. . . . —Hosea 10:12 (NIV)

There was always a garden at my house growing up. I remember watching and helping my mom and dad till the soil, chopping away overgrowth, including weeds and any unwanted shrubs. We would unearth worms and potato bugs, as we called them. And I loved the smell of freshly overturned dirt. There was something about it—maybe its smell reminded me of the potential of what could be planted and what could be produced. An expectation of what we would reap in its season. When harvest time came, we had okra, collards, spinach, turnips, and string beans. But before anything could be planted, we had to till. We had to break up the soil to prepare it for the sowing and the planting.

And it is the same with us. For the Word of the Lord to fall on good ground, the soil of our hearts must be prepared.

—Natasha N. Smith

Lord, continue to till the soil of my heart, so that I may receive all You have for me. Amen.

pivot

If my people, who are called by my name, will humble themselves and pray and seek my face and turn from their wicked ways, then I will hear from heaven, and I will forgive their sin and will heal their land. —2 Chronicles 7:14 (NIV)

My spiritual life is an ever-present process of being alert to the honest state of my heart and my soul—which, all too often, will wander astray. In those moments, I know that it is only by His help—and His strength, power, and wisdom—that any of these sins can be conquered.

That's when I pray: "Pivot."

For instance, have I noticed that I've grown too consumed with my work? "Lord, help me pivot and find ways to put my focus back on You." Have I neglected a certain responsibility in my life? "Lord, I want to pivot and recommit myself to that duty. What's one small way I can do that?"

Often it's these incremental, small changes—pivots—that ensure that I stay the course and stay connected to the Father who always pivots toward me.

—Elizabeth James

Lord, how can I pivot toward You today? I pray that You will lead and guide me and draw me closer to You in the process. Amen.

transplant

This is what the Lord God says, "I'm also going to take a shoot
from the top of a cedar and plant it . . . and it will grow
branches, bear fruit, and become a majestic cedar."
—Ezekiel 17:22–23 (ISV)

I frowned as I gently touched drooping stems and withered
leaves. My shamrock plant was not doing well at all.

"Maybe it could use a bigger pot," my friend suggested.

Should I transplant my shamrock? Being uprooted can be
difficult. It was possible it wouldn't survive the move. But the next
afternoon, I found a larger container in the shed and replanted
my shamrock. I smoothed fresh soil around the roots and set it in
a sunny window. Within just hours, the plant looked more vibrant. The next day, the droopy stems were standing up straight.

I thought of all the times God transplanted me . . . a new
job, a move, an unexpected change. They weren't always easy
but, with faith and hope, I always learned and grew. And now,
with more room for the roots to spread, my transplanted shamrock plant not only improved, but thrived.

—Peggy Frezon

God, help me to always thrive where You plant me.

challenge

Do not fear, for I am with you; do not be afraid, for I am your God. I will strengthen you; I will help you; I will hold on to you with my righteous right hand. —Isaiah 41:10 (CSB)

I stood before the wall and looked up. Ten feet looked like a thousand. Somehow, I was supposed to make it to the top so I could climb over to the other side. There was no way I could do this on my own. Thankfully, I didn't have to.

My team was there to help me with the obstacle course. One person boosted me from below while two teammates on top of the wall reached down to pull me up. This wall that seemed impossible was only a challenge. While I may not have been able to do it on my own, I could do it with the help around me.

When we face a challenge, we don't have to do it alone. God is there, giving us a boost and pulling us up to conquer what once felt impossible.

—Rebecca Hastings

Lord, help me see the hard things I face not as impossible,
but as challenges You help me overcome. Amen.

dignity

He blew into his nostrils the breath of life, and man became a living being. —Genesis 2:7 (JPS)

W hen she asked me how long she'd known me, I told her all my life, from the first kiss she'd given me on the day that I was born.

I'd lost my mom ten times over to Alzheimer's. Each lapse in her memory seemed to cut me away as if I'd never existed.

But I could do this. I could treat her with the dignity she deserved as a sweet human being; as a beloved, lost mother; as the once-competent woman who had birthed me.

I vowed to accept this version of my mom, the woman who had once taught me practical shopping tips but who now stuffed my head with silly songs, prattled on nonsensically, laughed at corny jokes, and was moved beyond words by a beautiful symphony.

I didn't really have a choice. But I made it anyway.

—Miriam Green

Dear God, Judaism teaches that we are all created in Your image. Help me remember that all people are deserving of being treated with dignity.

direct

The LORD directs the steps of the godly. He delights
in every detail of their lives. —Psalm 37:23 (NLT)

I once had an old car that would either die or refuse to start at
the most inconvenient moments. Outside the grocery store
with frozen food melting. A green light with horns blasting. A
train crossing. One day, it gasped an ugly sound that foretold the
end was near. And so, I began my quest for a "new" used car.

I had been earnestly praying for a specific luxury car, but
was in no position to buy it yet, so I didn't bother looking for
that model. I tirelessly searched for another car in my budget
the entire weekend, to no avail. Then I heard a small voice
chuckling, "What car have you been praying about every day
for the last three years?" With the excitement of a child, I
chugged into that high-end dealership and found out a retired
couple had *just* traded in their dated, yet perfectly beautiful,
sedan. It never made it to the showroom floor.

—Kimberly Shumate

*Father, I pray today that You direct me to Your blessings, in the
proper place at the proper time. Amen.*

equipped

All Scripture is God-breathed and is useful for teaching, rebuking, correcting and training in righteousness, so that the servant of God may be thoroughly equipped for every good work. —2 Timothy 3:16–17 (NIV)

Although I use a computer nearly every day, my ability to fix problems is a C-minus. So when the Delete feature stopped working and old email messages clogged my inbox, I was clueless. Friends offered suggestions for fixing the problem, but none of them worked. Finally, I did what I should have done first—I read the online instruction manual. Restoring the feature was quick and easy.

Sometimes the Delete feature in my mind quits working too; the focus of my attention shifts to me, myself, and I. When that happens, I turn to God's instruction book, the Bible. I read words of reproof and correction and words that help me reset my thoughts and priorities. Then I'm able to receive God's guidance and help in becoming equipped to do His work in the world.

—Penney Schwab

Lord Jesus, help me seek Your guidance each day
as I strive to do Your will.

steady

Make my steps steady through Your promise; don't let any sin dominate me. —Psalm 119:133 (HCSB)

When my children were in elementary school, I volunteered to chaperone a field trip that involved climbing the second tallest mountain in our state. The area had just experienced days of heavy rains, making the hiking trail a slick, muddy mess. As we ascended the mountain, our guide instructed us to climb slowly, making sure to maintain a good foothold with each movement.

For a group of fourth- and fifth-graders, this wasn't an easy task! Often, they wanted to move too quickly, which resulted in trips and slips. Even I fell victim to the desire to get to the top faster, and I came away with bruises to prove it.

A steady pace is crucial in our spiritual lives too. We often lack caution or try to move things along at a faster pace than God has set. However, God will steady our steps and support us as we follow Him.

—Elly Gilbert

Lord, steady our steps as we seek to follow You.

pure

Not mixed or adulterated with any other substance or material; without any extraneous and unnecessary elements; free of any contamination. —Oxford English Dictionary

M y refrigerator has a water purifying filter. I confess I can't honestly tell the difference between the purified water and what comes out of the tap, but I'm assured there's a big difference. The dictionary definition of the word tells me why. The filter removes stuff I don't want in there even if I can't see it. The filter removes everything that's . . . well, impure.

Jesus is the ultimate purifier. The Bible tells me that while sin sullies me through and through, in Christ, God sees me as brilliantly clean and totally pure. Even so, I know I'm still full of "extraneous and unnecessary elements" and "contamination." What a priceless blessing that Jesus doesn't leave me that way!

Over time and with my humble cooperation, Jesus filters out all my impurities, so that I more closely reflect His holy purity, a process completed in heaven.

—Isabella Campolattaro

Dear Jesus, thank You for purifying me by Your very blood and until I meet You face to face.

faithful

Let us hold fast the confession of our hope without wavering, for He who promised is faithful. —Hebrews 10:23 (NKJV)

Past due. Final notice. Back they went into the mailbox. I was a single mother, depending on God, and hard-pressed to cover gas and dog food with only $27. Still, I had to be diligent, keeping my thoughts on Him, not circumstances.

"Lord, please multiply my provision."

After getting gas, I was short for dog food, but it was nothing a coupon couldn't fix, if I had one: "Lord, You multiplied the fish and loaves—how about my seventeen dollars?"

Standing in faith, I placed the bag on the counter. The scanner beeped, and the cashier said, "Free."

My eyebrows rose. "R-e-a-l-l-y?"

He pointed to the screen. "Membership promotion. See?"

I thanked him, then practically floated to my car, giving God all the glory and praise.

—Pamela Hirson

Lord, teach me to be as faithful as You. Amen.

forget

I am he who blots out your transgressions for my own sake, and I will not remember your sins. —Isaiah 43:25 (ESV)

Both my husband and son live with some significant attention deficit quirks. It's a common occurrence in our home for Papa to place son in time-out for some misbehavior and set the timer to five minutes, at which point his plan is that they will talk. The timer goes off, my husband lovingly cuddles the boy, and asks, "Can you tell me why you had to have a time-out?" Our son shrugs. "I don't know. I forget."

At this point, my husband turns to me with panicked eyes, and I know exactly what this pleading expression is trying to convey—he has also forgotten. Whatever transgression transpired evaporated from their memories in that five-minute span as new thoughts and distractions flooded in.

I think these are the perfect example of "Godly time-outs." Before we are even done punishing ourselves or begging forgiveness, He says, "I forget. Let's talk about something else!"

—Sarah Greek

Lord, help me today to remember to forget my sins as quickly as You do! Amen.

climb

A hill is not too hard to climb/Taken one step at a time
—James Dillet Freeman, "One Step More"

I live in the Tennessee mountains. There's no place to walk, except on a treadmill, that doesn't involve climbing hills, and I thrive on it. Physical hill climbing is good for the legs, good for the lungs, good for the spirit. Figurative hill climbing is another story. Sometimes the everyday trials of life—from dealing with a leaky faucet to juggling appointments—seem to overwhelm me. Big trials are even worse.

In stressful times, be they little or large, I like to put on my shoes and go for a walk. As I climb the steep hill that leads from my house to the main road, I talk to God. His calming presence helps me plan how to break my seemingly insurmountable tasks into manageable steps. Half an hour and two hilly miles later, I'm ready to get the job done.

—Jennie Ivey

Remind me, Lord, that everything worthwhile is done
by small steps taken one by one.

teachable

Instruct the wise and they will be wiser still; teach
the righteous and they will add to their learning.
—Proverbs 9:9 (NIV)

My husband and I moved to North Africa thirty years ago, never dreaming we'd stay this long. When we first arrived, I had anticipated a time of learning to live and thrive in our new home, but what I discovered was a process of adaptation that has never ended.

Each morning I wake up ready to be taught something new about my host country, and it never fails. I recently learned that it is a tradition to offer an odd—never even—number of dates when welcoming guests.

How I wish I had approached life in the United States with the same attitude, ready to learn and be taught from the simple things happening every day. An open heart and an open mind create space in our lives for childlike learning that approaches every day with humility as well as adventure.

—Connie McDaniel

*Dear Lord, give me humility today as I place myself in a
teachable position with ears to hear and eyes to see. Amen.*

anticipation

Now faith is the substance of things hoped for,
the evidence of things not seen. —Hebrews 11:1 (KJV)

The State Fair was in town, and we were taking our grand-kids. I dreaded it. The overpriced rides. The games that were impossible to win. Greasy corn dogs and funnel cakes. The red dust of the Oklahoma wind. My bad knee throbbing in pain. This would be the worst day ever.

My grandson ran into the room and threw his arms around my legs. "I made us a snack bag, Grandma!" he said as he proudly held up a used Walmart bag overflowing with Little Debbie treats that he'd gathered from the pantry. "This is going to be the best day ever!"

I laughed at our differences in perspective and imagined the day through his eyes. The windswept hair while riding the swings. The delicious corn dogs and funnel cakes. The possibility of winning a stuffed teddy bear.

I lifted him in my arms. "It sure is!"

—Kristy Dewberry

*Father, my prayer today is that I begin to hope for and expect
Your blessings with a child's eager anticipation.*

message

I have a message from God in my heart . . .
—Psalm 36:1 (NIV)

My wife and I were newly married when I took a job working the 11 p.m. to 7 a.m. shift at a convenience store in northern Ohio. Each evening she fixed me a sack lunch and a gallon pitcher of sweet tea to fuel me through my shift. The sack lunch always contained a handwritten note, expressing her love and encouragement. I wish I'd saved those notes. They were brief and simple, but they meant a lot to me.

Something similar happens between me and God. Every morning and evening, I open a message of love and encouragement from Him as I read the Bible. Often I'll take a single word with me through the day. Sometimes a phrase, a sentence, or a verse. But His message always means a lot to me.

—Bob Hostetler

Lord, let a clear message from you be in my heart today. Amen.

jubilation

Splendor and majesty are before him; strength and joy are in his dwelling place. —1 Chronicles 16:27 (NIV)

There is one sound that can manifest pure joy in my household: the ice-cream truck rolling down our street. The kids leap up, grab their piggy banks, sprint for the yard, and chase down the slow-moving truck. It's a cause for much jubilation.

Once we get our ice creams, we grab spots on the lawn and watch the neighborhood sunset dipping into the treetops. In those perfect moments, the thin space where I can almost feel heaven on earth, we talk about our days, our troubles, and the things in our lives we're thankful for. It's in those thin spaces that I most like to talk about Jesus's love for us.

Think of the happiest you've ever been. Think how happy you feel right now, I say. That's how God feels when He looks down at you, His loved, chosen child.

—Ashley Kappel

Lord, help me find pure joy in the gifts You give me every day, from glowing sunsets to flowing rivers.

healing

But for you who revere my name, the sun of righteousness
will rise with healing in its rays. —Malachi 4:2 (NIV)

The MRI scan said I had multiple tears to my rotator cuff, which seemed to explain why I couldn't raise my left arm higher than my waist, and also why physical therapy had increased my pain.

My doctor referred me to the same surgeon who performed my husband's rotator cuff surgery. Remembering his monthslong recovery, I dreaded the inevitable. I didn't have time for this. I had things to do before our trip to Maui in ten weeks. I prayed for healing, and quickly!

The surgeon's next opening was three weeks away. Had God even heard my prayer? It became clear He had when the surgeon said I didn't need surgery. I had a frozen shoulder. A simple procedure would heal me in six weeks, not six months.

As I zip-lined on Maui six weeks later, I marveled at God's perfect healing.

—Linda L. Kruschke

*Dear Jesus, bring Your healing and hope to those waiting
in sickness and pain. Amen.*

receive

If you then, who are evil, know how to give good gifts to your children, how much more will your Father who is in heaven give good things to those who ask him! —Matthew 7:11 (ESV)

Scribbled on a paper leaf from our Thanksgiving tree were the words, "not getting internship." I paused, soaking in what that short phrase meant, and then breathed a quick prayer of thanks. My young adult son understood something I had long struggled with: The gifts God gives aren't always wrapped in pretty paper and topped with a bow.

A few months prior to our Thanksgiving celebration, our oldest child had been turned down for what seemed to be a perfect internship. It didn't make sense. But with grace belying his years, he received the ugly gift of rejection and began searching for new opportunities. Later that year, a door opened that eventually resulted in a full-time job he loved.

Despite his initial disappointment, my son realized God's sovereignty and His love for him. He reacted in faith, choosing to trust in God's goodness.

—Julie A. Sunne

Father, help me receive all You have for me with open hands, trusting that You know what's best for me.

mask

If you have a fault, be the first to say it.
—Talmud, Bava Kama 92B

I used to find it nearly impossible to recognize my own faults. Not that I spent a lot of time looking for them. It was as if I wore a pretty mask over them to keep anyone else (and therefore myself) from figuring out what was really hiding under there.

My journal from the year before I met my husband shows me clearly now who I was then—sarcastic, defensive, bitter, and hurting. Over the next twenty years, with my husband's unconditional love, I was able to admit those hurtful faults to myself, to grow into someone who understands the flaws in others because I can understand the flaws in myself.

Taking off the mask (and hanging it on the wall in case I needed it again) showed me who I really am—allowed me to let others see it too. Now, as I pray the word *mask*, I ask God to remind me that what I think of as my weaknesses can be my strength.

—Rhoda Blecker

Lord of honesty, even as I see my unmasked imperfections clearly now, please stick with me if I can't quite get them all fixed.

fading

May the God of green hope fill you up . . . with the life-giving energy of the Holy Spirit. —Romans 15:13 (MSG)

Why do you always close your drapes in the morning when you just opened them a few hours ago?" I'd seen my grandmother do this many times and wondered why. She answered, "To keep the sunlight from fading my furniture." It took years until I understood this concept—how the sun's rays could take the pigment out of the upholstery fabric. I learned it through experience, seeing the fading of various materials when left by a sunlit window too long.

Sometimes, life's troubles become the primary source of brightness in my world and make me feel like I'm fading, as though the vibrancy of my spirit has been sapped away. Life turns into a black-and-white movie in a technicolor world. But if I close the drapes on despair, let the Holy Spirit's light through, I can keep my spirit bright and full of life.

—Cathy Mayfield

When my soul is fading, Jesus, send the color
back with Your Spirit.

kaleidoscope

You are all one in Christ Jesus. —Galatians 3:28 (NIV)

When I was a child, my mother and I spent a lot of time searching for a name for the mysterious condition that kept me in constant pain. I missed quite a bit of school, but Mom always had something up her sleeve to create a teachable moment.

One morning in a doctor's waiting room, she reached deep inside her canvas tote. All eyes were on us as my Mary Poppins-mother pulled out cardboard tubes and passed them to everyone. "It's a kaleidoscope. Twist the knobs!" she urged the startled strangers. "What do you *see*?" All they saw was a bunch of broken glass in crazy colors moving around, the patterns constantly pulling from the outside toward the center.

"It's *us*!" Mom finally revealed. "That's all of our chairs wanting to scoot together." The entire room did just that. Mom's dime-store kaleidoscopes had performed their magic, bringing broken people together.

—Roberta Messner

Thank You for those who create a kaleidoscope
of caring in life's broken places.

sisu

Be diligent in these matters; give yourself wholly to them, so that everyone may see your progress. —1 Timothy 4:15 (NIV)

On a vintage dress form in our entry sits an authentic Finnish costume I inherited from my paternal grandmother, Edith Aspholm. Because I wrote the most letters to her during her lifetime, I won the costume contest she started when I was young. My mother says my determination to succeed shows I have *sisu.*

A word that expresses the national character of Finland, *sisu* has no English equivalent. It connotes stoic determination, tenacity of purpose, grit, bravery, resilience, and hardiness. I don't know that I have all those qualities, but my grandmother certainly did. She was a strong-minded Finn who raised her three sons alone during the Depression years after her husband died in a work-related accident. Those sons became successful businessmen . . . perhaps because of *sisu.* I pray that I also pursue God's purpose for my life with that same kind of passion.

—Janet Holm McHenry

Lord, develop the kind of grit in me that helps see me through hard times and the varied challenges of life.

hear

My sheep hear my voice, and I know them,
and they follow me. —John 10:27 (KJV)

So many voices call to us in this world. Voices of commercials, careers, finances, household chores, family, friends, and hobbies. By the end of the day, we have heard so many voices we can't hear the Lord.

Still, He continues to call. Sometimes it's barely a whisper. Yet it's that soft tone that gets our attention. Like a distressed child who's crying and cannot hear their parent's voice until they whisper gently, "Hush, sweet child. I am here."

In the busyness of life, I long to perceive God's calming voice in my ear. I know Him. I'm familiar with His voice—it's like no other. But I must make time to be still and listen for it. Oh, the sweet peace that settles my spirit when I block out the world and hear God's voice.

—Tez Brooks

*Kind Shepherd, speak to me today. Teach me to hear
Your voice that I might follow only You. Amen.*

hollow

Who has measured the waters of the sea in the hollow of his hand? —Isaiah 40:12 (NRSVUE)

ook what I found!" my wife called to me as she was weeding her garden. It was a rabbit nest hidden in the pachysandra. The mama bunny had dug out a hollow and lined it with soft grass, pine needles, and bits of fur. And now there were five babies—kittens, they're called—all snuggled together, safe and secure from foxes and hawks. "You stay in your little hollow," Mary said to the kittens. "You'll be safe down there."

A hollow is a place of safety and security. I remember a hymn chorus from my childhood, "In the hollow of His hand! In the hollow of His hand! I am safe, whatever may betide me, in the hollow of His hand!"* To this day, when I am feeling frightened or insecure, I will find myself praying, "Lord, hold me in the hollow of Your hand."

—Lou Lotz

Lord, hold me in the hollow of Your hand. Amen.

---

*"With my Saviour ever near to guide me," music by Edmund Simon Lorenz, in *Hymns New and Old, No. 2* (New York: Fleming H. Revell, 1890).

humbled

Do nothing out of selfish ambition or vain conceit.
Rather, in humility value others above yourselves . . .
—Philippians 2:3 (NIV)

M any years ago, I went on a mission trip to Bolivia with my church. I was looking forward to God using me to help. One of the stops in Bolivia was a visit to one of the local's homes for a church service. The family lived in a house built out of cinder blocks. This home was in the mountains, and the other local church members walked for miles in open-toed sandals across the jagged rocks. One of the women who had arrived asked for prayer for her bleeding feet. Another woman took up her carrots for the offering.

My life was changed forever by witnessing the dedication of the Bolivian people. I had gone there thinking I would help them, but I was the one who was helped. They showed me that material things don't matter compared to the peace and joy they found in the love of God.

—Amanda Pennock

God, may I never think of myself better than anyone else. Help me not to do anything out of selfish ambition or vain conceit.

precious

There is gold and abundance of costly stones, but the lips of knowledge are a precious jewel. —Proverbs 20:15 (ESV)

When I read or hear the word *precious*, I often think of the *Lord of the Rings* trilogy. The eponymous ring's power ensnares the character Gollum and he repeatedly refers to it as "my precious." He's captivated by its allure.

The story challenges me to think about what is *my* "precious." What holds me spellbound and occupies my time and thoughts?

Every morning, coffee is my precious. My children, whom I adore, can be my precious too. As a devout bargain shopper, I'm consumed by finding the best prices; great deals are precious to me.

Those things aren't bad necessarily, but in the economy of God, their value pales in comparison. To Him, wisdom and knowledge are precious. Thankfully, when I'm focused on God, He changes my desires to align with His.

—Robin Dance

Lord, help me to want wisdom more than anything the world can offer.

though

Though the fig tree does not bud and there are no grapes on the vines . . . yet I will rejoice in the LORD, I will be joyful in God my Savior. —Habakkuk 3:17–18 (NIV)

Watching the nightly news and reading the book of Habakkuk can feel eerily similar: the ongoing corruption, rampant diseases, violent acts of nature, war, and disregard for goodness. Habakkuk experiences the same in Judah. He's perplexed that God allows wickedness, strife, and oppression to run rampant and does nothing. He demands to know "Why?" and "How long?"

God gives a surprising answer. His plan goes contrary to everything Habakkuk has believed to this point. But Habakkuk finally grows quiet and still. He listens, even *though* he doesn't understand. The book ends with his decision to praise God even *though* nothing has changed. He doesn't need answers. He needs only to rejoice. I, too, need to take all my questions to God and then rejoice, even *though*.

—Terrie Todd

God, I lay all my own "thoughs" at Your feet. I choose to rejoice and praise You, even though. *Amen.*

breath

The Spirit of God has made me; the breath of the
Almighty gives me life. —Job 33:4 (NIV)

As a child, I often held my breath whenever I was nervous or frightened, completely unaware of what I was doing until dizziness overtook me or someone reminded me to breathe. Though I outgrew that habit, until I found my way to Jesus, unpaid bills, health challenges, and unresolved conflicts seemed to smother my dreams. He alone rescued me, breathing life into my empty existence.

Today, as I write at my desk, I appreciate the profound value of being alive. Just outside my window, the sun shines and leaves dance on the wind. Birds perform an aerial ballet for me. Like the breath of dawn, fresh hope is born through His grace daily. His breath fills creation, and it responds with joy. I take a deep breath, grateful and blessed.

—Heidi Gaul

*God, thank You. Every breath I take is a blessing
from You, and I am grateful. Amen.*

yoke

Take My yoke upon you and learn from Me, for I am gentle
and lowly in heart, and you will find rest for your souls.
—Matthew 11:29 (NKJV)

I have an antique wooden yoke that hangs in my house as décor, an inheritance from my mother. I seize teachable moments when my grandchildren ask questions about it, explaining that a yoke is used for harnessing oxen to enable them to pull heavy loads together, easing their work. And so it is with our Lord. When we submit wholly to Christ, we are yoked to Him. Jesus promises that when we stay with Him, He will lift the heavy burden of trying to earn our way into heaven. The yoke of Jesus is gentle and lowly, with only one commitment—to follow Him.

My antique yoke is laced with splinters. Christ's yoke is laced with grace, liberty, and rest. It provides us all that we really need, making our work so much lighter.

—Becky Van Vleet

*Lord, thank You for the yoke You provide for us when
our souls are weary, so we can rest with You.*

bejeweled

Everyone who competes in the games goes into strict training. They do it to get a crown that will not last, but we do it to get a crown that will last forever. —1 Corinthians 9:25 (NIV)

My turn, my turn." My daughters fought over a shiny plastic gold crown with purple, green, and red stickers for jewels. With their aggressive play, the crown only lasted a few hours.

In contrast, God bestows eternal crowns in heaven. When I'm having a hard time administering grace to a troublesome person, I remind myself that God views this as an opportunity to be bejeweled. When I refuse to compromise on His command to love one another even in almost impossible situations, He administers His reward. Is it a jewel? I don't know, but it certainly puts a smile on my face. I touch my head and say "bling" as I walk away from a rough encounter, knowing I showed God's grace and love.

Go about gathering eternal rewards. Encourage yourself by saying, "Bling, another jewel in my incorruptible crown."

Image bearer of God, be bejeweled today.

—Heather Roberts

Lord Jesus, teach me to abundantly display Your love to all people, so that I might bring You joy in my obedience. Amen.

freedom

So if the Son sets you free, you will be free indeed.
—John 8:36 (NIV)

I loved flying kites as a kid. My dad would bring us four girls a kite home, and we would be so excited that he could hardly assemble it. I remember when it was time to fly it, I held the kite up against the wind, just enough for the air to catch underneath and begin to lift it. I started to release the string from my hand, a little at a time, until the kite began to soar. Then I started to run, looking up at the kite as it flew freely in the sky.

I believe we are the kite when we find freedom in Christ. We catch the wind and are lifted from the weight of heavy burdens, and then we begin to soar on wings like eagles. Although life is not void of problems, there is freedom in knowing we never have to face life alone. God is always there to lift us up.

—Natasha N. Smith

Lord, I pray that I will forever abide in Your freedom. Amen.

graft

I am the vine; you are the branches. If you remain in me and I in you, you will bear much fruit; apart from me you can do nothing. —John 15:5 (NIV)

Gardening is a favorite hobby of mine, so I have learned a lot about what it takes to grow a bountiful garden—including the art of grafting. It is generally done with plants, such as apple trees, by attaching the root from one variety to the upper stem of another. The two grow together, combining the best of both varieties so that the resulting plant is better than either of the originals.

There are similarities to this grafting in my spiritual walk as well. I must ensure that I'm always firmly attached to His roots. That means coming back, again and again, and praying this word over myself, my heart, and my day. Unlike the apple trees in my yard who must only be grafted once, spiritual grafting is a process that I must tend to in prayer, day after day.

—Elizabeth James

Lord, graft me to Yourself! Show me, today, how to remain in You and show me the ways that I might try to resist that. I want to always grow in You. Amen.

gray

Gray hair is a crown of splendor; it is attained in the way
of righteousness. —Proverbs 16:31 (NIV)

G ray clouds on a spring day, gray roots on her scalp, and
gray feelings that come from depression. I would have
described my aging mother as feeling gray: not only was
she experiencing withdrawal from nicotine and one of her medi-
cations at the same time, but she was also wrestling with grief on
the one-year anniversary of her youngest son's death. Gray. It's a
lingering, heavy emotion, and she doesn't want to get out of bed.

I encouraged her to consider the fatigue from a different perspective. Perhaps God is allowing her to sleep while He rids her of
toxic chemicals. Her body is healing from the substances, but also
the sorrow. God loves her and He's showing her mercy. Mom's life
hasn't been completely righteous—nobody's is. But Jesus, in His
all-encompassing love, offers new mercies every morning.

I remind Mom that she is the daughter of the King of Kings.
She smiles while pinning up her crown of long, gray hair.

—Kelly Fordyce Martindale

*Lord, thank You for our elders, who continue to teach us
that life is precious regardless of the weather outside.*

ordinary

A woman from Samaria came to draw water. "Give me
a drink," Jesus said to her. —John 4:7 (CSB)

I t wasn't anything new or exciting. Another night of making
dinner and giving baths, of bedtime stories and even sibling
squabbles. It was what I did every day.

Sometimes everyday life can start to feel boring, so much
so that we wonder if God is even in those places. We know He's
there on a Sunday morning in worship or even during some of the
hardest trials we walk through. But what about on ordinary days?

Remember the woman gathering water at the well in John 4?
She was doing her daily chores, nothing noteworthy, and she
had one of the most famous interactions with Jesus in the
whole Bible. Jesus met her in the middle of her ordinary day.
Just like He did for that woman at the well, God meets us
everywhere, even in our ordinary places.

—Rebecca Hastings

Father, thank You for meeting me in my ordinary life.
Show me more of Your presence in all I do. Amen.

seek

Seek his will in all you do . . . — Proverbs 3:6 (NLT)

C an you remember playing hide-and-seek as a kid? One person would cover their eyes and count to one hundred while the others would run and hide. "Ready or not, here I come," the counter would call as they began their search. I remember how some kids would search and search until they found every playmate, while others would seek for a while and then give up because it was just too hard.

I'm struck by the word *seek* today. There have been times, in relationships and jobs, when I've found it challenging to wait on God's will. The question becomes: Am I like the child who will continue seeking His will with patience and perseverance? Or am I like the child who finds it too hard and gives up? I want God's will in all I do. So, I must seek it.

—Kara Plett

Father, today, please draw my attention to what I am seeking,
and, when I become impatient, help me to seek after
Your will with perseverance.

cake

Be rich in good deeds, and . . . be generous
and willing to share. —1 Timothy 6:18 (NIV)

I t took two city buses from Hollywood to reach Beverly Hills, where I worked. The differences between the areas was startling. Like clockwork each morning, I would greet Duane, a homeless guy who was a fixture in a doorway near my job. He looked so out of place.

Months passed, and Christmas came. And though he had no possessions except the ones he carried, Duane handed me a beautifully wrapped cake that an affluent housewife had given him. I stood there, dumbfounded, trying my best to refuse the gift. *Here is a man with nothing. How can I accept?* But Duane beamed as he insisted that I take it and enjoy it.

With all the "cake" in this world—wealth, power, glamour, luxury—and with so many people who don't have any, I will always remember the generosity of one very rich man in particular.

—Kimberly Shumate

*God, bless those who share cake, and may I learn to share
and to accept the gift joyfully. Amen.*

steadfast

They will have no fear of bad news; their hearts are steadfast, trusting in the Lord. —Psalm 112:7 (NIV)

D uring a routine checkup, my doctor detected a slight heartbeat irregularity. It wasn't an emergency, he said, so I'd have to wait to see a cardiologist. After a moment's thought, he asked how much coffee I drank. When I confessed to having five-plus cups each morning, he suggested I cut consumption by two-thirds, call immediately if I felt unwell, and have another electrocardiogram in a month.

I was mostly comfortable with that plan, but I found myself checking my pulse often. Then I received a card with Psalm 112:7 printed on the back. I remembered that the word *steadfast* meant firm and unwavering. So I prayed for steadfast trust that God would take away my uneasiness about what was happening with my heart.

The repeat electrocardiogram was normal. I left the office with three blessings: a steady heartbeat, better health from reduced caffeine intake, and a new appreciation of the peace that comes with steadfast trust.

—Penney Schwab

Lord, thank You for keeping me more steadfast in all of life's situations.

tenderhearted

Instead, be kind to each other, tenderhearted, forgiving
one another, just as God through Christ has forgiven you.
—Ephesians 4:32 NLT

Her harsh words stung my heart. Nursing my hurt feelings, I let anger bubble up. How dare she say such cruel things to me? As I plotted ways to return the hurt, my heart began to harden toward my offender.

The next morning, I read Ephesians 4:32 during my quiet time: "Instead, be kind to each other, tenderhearted, forgiving one another . . ." (NLT). My heart had certainly been tender when her words pierced it, but my response allowed anger and bitterness to make it calloused.

To enjoy the forgiveness Christ offers me, I needed to forgive my offender and let my heart be tender again—something I can only do through the grace and power of God.

—Elly Gilbert

Father, make my heart tender and kind toward others.
Help me forgive so that I can be forgiven. Amen.

metanoia

*A person convinced against their will is of the
same opinion still.* —Unknown

The Greek word *metanoia* is rich with meaning, a precious revelation for the Christian life. Metanoia means a transformative change of heart born of sincere sorrow and regret. I know this feeling! It seems the longer I've been a Christian, the more quickly I feel the discomfort of sin and knowing I'm out of sync with God's heart. Not faking it, but feeling it and responding.

Metanoia calls to mind Psalm 51:17, which explains that God doesn't want sacrifices or offerings when we sin. He wants broken hearts. Does this sound cruel? It's really not. God knows that as we draw ever closer to Him, we will feel the pain of destructive sin and turn away from it to embrace the heart of love for our own good.

The searing pain of knowing how we've hurt ourselves, others, or God's spirit is the catalyst for true metanoia, heart change. That's what the Lord wants for us . . . because He loves us so.

—Isabella Campolattaro

Dear Jesus, may metanoia help me become ever more like You!

chat

Every good conversation starts with a good listener.
—Unknown

I really like sleeping. My children have never felt the same way. The oldest, who is brilliantly neurodivergent, has a brain that won't stop. We often hear his door creak open at some dark-o'clock hour and his scampering steps down the hall until he snuggle-crashes next to me and whispers in the loudest possible way, "Hey, Mom! You want to chat about surface tension or astrophysics?!"

No. No, I really do not. I love his whimsical wonder, but mercy, I want to sleep! I can't even remember English words at that hour, let alone have a "chat" about the things he wants to dissect.

I'm very grateful that God doesn't have my human short-comings. Any midnight hour—literally any time our hearts or minds have a thought we want to share or process—He is there listening, ready to chat. And He promises not to doze off!

—Sarah Greek

Thank You, Lord, that You are available to me anytime, anywhere, and genuinely care to hear what I have to say. Amen.

return

... for the LORD your God is gracious and compassionate.
He will not turn his face from you if you return to him.
—2 Chronicles 30:9 (NIV)

Watching the tips of our poplar trees outside the living-room window, I realize the tiny birds dancing amid the branches are smaller than our regular visitors. They are busier than the sparrows or chickadees that visit our feeders each morning. One glimpse through the binoculars confirms my hope: yellow-rumped warblers have returned! They are the first migrating bird species to arrive this spring. Like many other species we wait for each spring, these birds return like clockwork. They know where to find food, shelter, and everything they need for their impressive voyages.

Witnessing their return, I feel God's promptings—like migrational signals to a bird—to return to His refuge. I circle back to prayer, fellowship, and well-worn passages of Scripture He uses to refresh my spirit. Returning to His presence, I find all I need for the journey.

—Eryn Lynum

Dear Lord, prompt me back to Your presence, that I may return time and again to Your tender care and faithful provisions. Amen.

found

Or suppose a woman has ten silver coins and loses one. Doesn't she light a lamp, sweep the house and search carefully until she finds it? —Luke 15:8 (NIV)

M y friend lost a strawberry.

Not a big deal, right? She still had a whole bowlful. But she swore she'd heard it go *plop* as it dropped on the floor and was concerned that her cat—the one with violent food allergies—would find it first.

So she looked on the floor. Nothing. She moved the dish around. Got on her hands and knees, scouring every inch of the kitchen from a cat's-eye view. Still nothing.

In desperation, she murmured a quick prayer. "Lord, I know it's just a strawberry, but I need Your help. Will You please show me where it is?" And—you guessed it—her eye immediately went to a corner, where she saw the renegade red fruit.

Coincidence? Perhaps. But to her, this small blessing was an intimate expression of God's love that sent her faith soaring.

—Leslie McLeod

Lord, thank You for using everyday things to help us find our way to You. Amen.

goodwill

Do not plot harm against your neighbor, who lives trustfully near you. —Proverbs 3:29 (NIV)

I own an eBay business. Every morning, I put my sold items on the front porch for our mail carrier to pick up. We had heard stories about people stealing packages right off others' porches, and my husband installed a camera so I could keep watch from my iPad.

One day I glanced at my iPad and saw my new neighbor in the driveway holding a shipping box. He and three other college kids had rented the house across the street. I had been wary when they moved in, anticipating late-night parties and loud music, although there had been no problems yet. I grabbed my cell phone and rushed out the door to catch him in the act.

The "act" that I caught him in was delivering a package for me that had been left on their porch by mistake. Fortunately, I realized my error before making a complete fool of myself.

—Kristy Dewberry

Father, today I pray that my heart be full of goodwill toward others. Forgive me for the times I misjudge those around me. Help me to assume the best of others instead of the worst.

meek

. . . where meek souls will receive him, still the dear Christ enters in. —Phillips Brooks, "O Little Town of Bethlehem"

I remember Doug and his wife entering the first church I pastored. He was six foot five and bearded. Broad-shouldered. Strong. Imposing in appearance. A few weeks after first walking into that church, Doug bowed his hulking form in prayer and received "the dear Christ" into his heart and life. Soon, he was driving the church van and herding scores of children here and there with a humility, patience, gentleness, and self-control that defines for me the word *meek*.

It's unfortunate that *meek* rhymes with *weak*; that makes it too easy to associate one with the other. I pray for a faith like Doug's. Today I will pray it repeatedly in a single word: *meek*. I'll never be as tall, as strong, or as imposing as Doug, but I will ask God to fill my soul with "the meekness and gentleness of Christ" (2 Corinthians 10:1, KJV).

—Bob Hostetler

*God, please help me to reflect the meekness
of Christ throughout this day. Amen.*

exquisite

And so we know and rely on the love God has for us.
God is love. Whoever lives in love lives in God,
and God in them. —1 John 4:16 (NIV)

Raising elementary-school girls is hard. Research shows that around age nine, they begin to lose their confidence, and their spark can wane. I'm on a one-woman quest to turn that around for the girls in my daughter's third-grade class.

I'm in a lucky position; I'm both a Girl Scout leader and a Bible Club host for our grade, which means I'm around these girls at least five or six times a month. Each time I go to one of these meetings, I pick a word and try to make it stick with them for the day.

When I read the research about turning nine, I knew I had to make it part of the lesson. I prayed over the word *exquisite*, taught them each what it meant, and told them they are perfect creations of a God who loves them, no matter what, forever. And that they should never let anyone tell them otherwise or make them feel any less.

—Ashley Kappel

*Lord, remind me to see myself through Your eyes
and leave harsh judgments behind.*

dependence

My salvation and my honor depend on God; he is
my mighty rock, my refuge. —Psalm 62:7 (NIV)

My son's high school had an alternating class schedule: four classes on A-day and four on B-day. One winter, a snowstorm closed school. The next day, my son discovered he had taken the wrong books because the school changed the regular schedule. He called before I left for work to ask if I would bring him the correct books.

When I walked into the school office, the secretary scolded me. "These kids need to learn responsibility, to be independent," she said. "He'll never learn if you bail him out." What she didn't realize was that I preferred he learn dependence.

In a world that runs on the mentality of pulling yourself up by your bootstraps, God honors those who depend on Him. We were created to be in relationship with God and others. At twenty-seven, my son still asks me for help and advice. I am thankful he learned that he can depend on me.

—Linda L. Kruschke

Dear Jesus, thank You for being my rock and refuge,
the One I can always depend on. Amen.

savor

But thanks be to God, who always puts us on display in Christ and through us spreads the aroma of the knowledge of Him in every place. —2 Corinthians 2:14 (HCSB)

Each morning I arise, eager to tackle my to-do list, looking to glorify God in these daily tasks. Yet in my focus on doing, I often miss Him: His grace and love, His countless moment-by-moment gifts. It's certainly not intentional. My drive to meet my obligations simply gets in the way of glorifying God. I forget to delight in the moment, to savor the gift of now.

A life lived in Christ is about abiding, not performing. But sometimes the striving gets in the way of the thriving. So, I stop and remind myself to notice the daily gifts: a steaming cup of tea, a brilliant red sky, my daughter's chuckle, the caress of a soft breeze, the warmth of home, and love of family. Amid my tasks I seek to celebrate the day God created and filled with blessings just for me.

—Julie A. Sunne

Lord, help me notice the glory in each day, the big moments and the myriad of small daily gifts, to delight in all You have graced me with. Amen.

community

Do not separate yourself from the community. —Rabbi Hillel

I'm an introvert, one of those people who doesn't mind if some meeting I was supposed to attend gets canceled. But a month after my husband, Keith, died, when I was through the mourning into the grief, one of my friends said, "My advice is that anytime someone asks you to do something, say yes."

At first I thought that was a terrible idea. I wanted to just pull in my emotions and squirrel myself at home with the dog and the cats. But when the synagogue needed my help with the newsletter, I said yes, and I discovered that helping them helped me. Finally I understood what my friend had been telling me. Being part of the community gave me a purpose that seclusion could not.

Later, when COVID-19 hit, I put that lesson to good use. I was more than ready to be an active member of several different virtual communities, embracing that sense of purpose even when I was home alone.

—Rhoda Blecker

Thank You for Zoom at exactly the time so many of us needed it.

essence

This is how we know that we live in him and he in us:
He has given us of his Spirit. —1 John 4:13 (NIV)

Who knew that Julius Caesar and Aristotle would agree about the essence of life? Caesar said, "Creativity is the essence of life." Aristotle, "The energy of the mind is the essence of life." I believe "creativity" and "the energy of the mind" are synonymous. It certainly is for me and other artists.

The dictionaries say "essence" is the important part of something. For a writer or sculptor, creative energy brings out the essence of who they are, the all-important piece of their makeup . . . their life itself. I know it to be true for me.

And yet I think I need to dig deeper, past the dictionary definitions, past the theories of Julius Caesar and Aristotle. Who I am—the core essence of my being—does indeed come from creativity, but that essence would be naught without God. I'm thankful He's placed the essence of His Spirit in me and all His children, regardless of their gifts or vocations.

—Cathy Mayfield

You in me, and I in You—this is my true essence. Thank You, Jesus.

wind

God is spirit, and his worshipers must worship
in the Spirit and in truth. —John 4:24 (NIV)

Today's too windy to go kayaking," my husband said. I looked out the window and saw the trees gently swaying. The lake behind our house rippled as if it had a current. The wind chimes hanging from our back porch were ringing. I hadn't stepped outside my house yet, but what I saw confirmed my husband's comment.

Funny thing about wind. You can't see it, but you can see its effect on other objects. The Bible says God is Spirit, and you can't see Him, but like the wind, you can see the effect He has on others. I know because I have seen and felt His effect in my life.

—Marilyn Turk

Lord, thank You for being there, even though I can't see You.

curate

You are the light of the world. A town built on a hill
cannot be hidden. —Matthew 5:14 (NIV)

W hile wandering through an antiques mall, I noticed a frail, white-haired woman trailing behind. "You pick up the best things every time," she said. "Are you a museum curator?"

"Nah," I assured her. "Just a hopeless junker." As I slowed my steps to hers, we visited the rest of the booths together. She was an expert on Navajo jewelry; I commented on the luscious colors and applique work of a nineteenth-century Baltimore Album quilt. Later we sat together on a sofa sipping hot tea. "I think that quilt belongs in a museum," I told her.

"I *knew* you were a curator!" she said, smiling. "I didn't descend from royalty, but I know a crown when I see one!"

God had sent a stranger to curate *me*—to show me the hidden details that make me more valuable than I realized.

—Roberta Messner

Master Curator, thank You for seeing things
in me I can't see myself.

mystery

To them God has chosen to make known among the Gentiles the glorious riches of this mystery, which is Christ in you, the hope of glory. —Colossians 1:27 (NIV)

I love murder mysteries. Not the gory, bloody kind. The cozy ones that take place in an old Victorian house or an Egyptian desert with no way to escape the murderer. When I figure out whodunit before the book or movie ends, I laugh with a sense of triumph.

My relationship with God is a different kind of mystery. The mystery of Christ in me. When I said yes to God's offer of a new life, Jesus stepped inside my heart. Wow. Sometimes I forget He's there and try to do life on my own. That never works. But when I remember Jesus lives in me—a mystery I can't yet fully grasp—I ask for His help. And He's never failed me yet.

—Jeanette Levellie

*Dear Jesus, my heart swells with hope when
I ponder the mystery of You living in me!*

calm

. . . and the peace of God, which surpasses all understanding, will guard your hearts and minds through Christ Jesus. —Philippians 4:7 (NKJV)

I n front of me is nothing but blinding, eerie gray. The New England valley through which I am traveling is shrouded in fog. With my foot scarcely pressing the accelerator, I creep forward anxiously, hoping the way will be revealed. Anxiety and worry arrive unbidden. What if a deer or a moose appears out of the fog? What if the road suddenly takes a sharp turn and I am unable to maneuver it?

These fearful thoughts are still swirling through my heart and mind when I ascend out of the valley and up the mountainside. The fog evaporates, and I find myself in brilliant sunlight. The scene from this perspective is calming and safe. Here, the haunting, gray fog becomes a soft, white blanket hovering over the valley, as if protecting it. What I anxiously perceived as something to be feared appears from this higher perspective beautiful and calm.

—Renee Joy Janzen

Lord, instead of worrying, I'm praying. Replace my worry with a calm that goes beyond understanding.

skill

I have filled him with the Spirit of God, with wisdom, with understanding, with knowledge and with all kinds of skills.
—Exodus 31:3 (NIV)

Throughout my life I've been an actor, singer, and writer. God also entrusted me with the responsibility of husband, father, leader, and teacher. In each of those roles I've struggled with feelings of inadequacy, comparing myself to others. It's caused me to sacrifice awards, responsibility, even income. More tragically, my insecurity has forfeited blessings—to me and others.

People often struggle with "imposter syndrome." It's the fear that others will discover that we are not as learned, talented, or skilled as we portray. This false thinking gnaws inside us, diminishing the value we bring to the world.

In reality, God bestows gifts upon us, fully equipping each of us to move in that ability and know-how. When we utilize our skills with confidence, we bless others and elevate Him.

—Tez Brooks

Lord, help me use the skills You've given me to glorify You. Amen.

refocus

Be still, and know that I am God! —Psalm 46:10 (NRSVUE)

Walking in my woods one morning, I saw a metallic green bug go skittering across a fallen log. It was a six-spotted tiger beetle looking for breakfast— small spiders, ants, whatever prey will fit in its mandibles. Tiger beetles are such fast runners that their sight can't keep up with their speed, so they run blind, this way and that, not really knowing where they are going. Now and then they have to stop and let their eyes refocus before they go charging off again.

Sometimes I find myself rushing through life at such a fast pace that I don't think about where I am going or why. I don't really notice the people around me or savor this sweet life. I look, but I don't see. I listen, but I don't hear. So I need to stop, take a deep breath, and speak a one-word prayer—refocus.

—Lou Lotz

Eternal God, help me to slow down, to refocus.

whenever

Whenever the cloud lifted from above the tent,
the Israelites set out; wherever the cloud settled,
the Israelites encamped. —Numbers 9:17 (NIV)

I felt a nudge to go outside and sit with her during our lunch break. I listened to her story as she opened her heart, shared about her struggles. She'd almost left the room during the discussion. The class was getting hard, dealing with past hurts. I had almost stayed inside during the break, but felt led to step outside, then sit next to the one who had sat behind me in class. God used me in that moment to encourage her.

The Israelites knew when to set out because they had a clear and distinct sign from God. "Whenever" reminds us to always seek God's timing, and look for the signs of when to proceed. Whenever prompted to pray for someone. Whenever spurred to step out in faith. Whenever invited to listen. Whenever God moves and we sense His leading.

—Susan Brehmer

*Lord, may I be observant to Your leading whenever
You call me to move. Amen.*

whatever

Finally, brothers, whatever is true, whatever is honorable,
whatever is just . . . think about these these things.
—Philippians 4:8 (ESV)

When my children were younger, there was one response sure to infuriate me: *"What . . . ever . . ."* Invariably, it meant they didn't like something I had said or suggested, and it carried a tone of disrespect that wasn't acceptable. I'd often overreact rather than gently correct. But God found a way to take a triggering word and make it beautiful to me.

It came by way of a fifth-grade bulletin board and an imaginative teacher. Using construction paper, cut-out letters, and oodles of creativity, Mrs. Heyworth created a showstopping bulletin board using Philippians 4:8 for inspiration. Rather than a negative expression, "whatever" was connected to *positive* words.

The visual inspired me to pray whatever was true, honorable, just, pure, lovely, and commendable over my children for a heavenly minded attitude adjustment . . . theirs and mine.

—Robin Dance

Lord, help me and those I love to dwell on whatever
You say is excellent and worthy of praise. Amen.

same

Jesus Christ is the same yesterday and today and forever.
—Hebrews 13:8 (ESV)

Have you been disappointed? Has something or *someone* changed unexpectedly?

Most of us answer yes to this. Sometimes we are desperate for something we can count on to stay the same.

Sometimes we need a reminder that Jesus does.

For over fifty years our family has vacationed at a rugged stretch of beach along the Oregon Coast. After the five-hour drive, my heart relaxes when I spot an enormous landmark rising up from the sand and waves. Haystack Rock—with its impressive size and unique shape—is exactly as I remember. Its constancy brings me peace.

Looking up at Haystack helps me to remember that Jesus is our everlasting rock—the only one that will never crumble into the sea.

No matter what we are experiencing, Jesus brings us peace. In the ordinary and in the overwhelming, we can look to Him and rest in His steadfast presence and unchanging love.

—Susie Crosby

Dear Jesus, You are the only absolute, sure thing in my life. Thank You that I can always count on You to stay the same. Amen.

align

Teach me to do your will, for you are my God; may your good Spirit lead me on level ground. —Psalm 143:10 (NIV)

D oes my car need a wheel alignment? How often should I see my chiropractor to keep my spine properly aligned? With which belief system or political party do I align myself? Will I go bonkers if the pictures hanging on my wall do not neatly align with one another? Do I want to use left, right, or center alignment on this document?

The idea of alignment faces us in practical ways every day, but far more important questions need asking. Is my will in alignment with God's? Are my actions aligned with His purposes? A productive Christian life involves aligning ourselves with God's plan in big and small ways, every day. When we trust God to align us, we become far less likely to stray from the path He has set us on. Align me, Lord. Align me.

—Terrie Todd

Lord, teach me to align myself to Your will
every moment of every day. Amen.

bigger

Take delight in the LORD, and he will give you the desires
of your heart. —Psalm 37:4 (NIV)

'␣ve just returned from my weekly shopping for fruits and vege-
tables. As I unpacked them, I couldn't ignore how much bigger
the produce is than when I was a child. They've mushroomed,
like supersized fast-food meals, oversized houses, and my hips.

At some point I began desiring more and bigger things. My
wants became needs, and then bigger needs.

I had to change, to refocus on the desires of my heart. Now
I eat just half of the gigantic apple and find satisfaction in my
cozy, perfect-for-two cottage. And I love me, no matter the size
of my wallet or my body.

My true needs can only be filled by Someone who is bigger
than anything this world provides—God. Faith in Him brings
eternal treasures and a love greater than I can imagine. This
need is the deepest desire of my heart.

—Heidi Gaul

God, help me keep my oversized wants aligned with
the bigger treasures You provide.

day

This is the day which the LORD hath made; we will rejoice and be glad in it. —Psalm 118:24 (KJV)

Adorned in a princess dress, furry pink slippers, and jewelry galore, my three-year-old daughter, Meredith, was ready to face the day. She entered our dining room with her beautiful smile and joyfully requested breakfast—with a tea party, too, of course. She happily awaited her royal breakfast of pancakes, syrup, and "tea." Meredith gladly started each new day dressed in her sparkly best.

As Christians I wonder if we lose the excitement and joy for each new day. Do we face the day looking for examples of God's goodness and blessings? The evidence of His blessings is all around us: sharing a smile with a neighbor, witnessing the beauty of nature, and enjoying the love of our families. We can experience the fullness of life each day as we open our physical and spiritual eyes to the wonders of God.

—Dawn Bata

Dear Lord, thank You for the gift of each new day. Amen.

gonflé

I am the way and the truth and the life. —John 14:6 (NIV)

Gonflé, from the French, means inflated, swollen, insolent. Untranslatable, it's *all* of these.

People who are *gonflé* are inflated from within like a cloud (Ecclesiastes 11:3). They are swollen from ungodly thoughts. Their insolence comes from anger carried deep in their souls.

I take *gonflé* very seriously. I cannot let lack of forgiveness swell me up so that—like a facelift gone bad—I'm no longer recognizable as God's child. I cannot let my finely tuned connection with God be burst by not giving credit to the Holy Spirit for my accomplishments. I cannot refuse God's help without hitting a brick wall of insolence, not trusting God's plan.

Jesus is not *gonflé*. He holds me tenderly in His arms, dries my tears, and whispers, now that I am listening, what His way is.

—Mayra Fernandez

All these gonflé *examples I describe above, Jesus, I am guilty of and more. Thank You, Holy Spirit, for leading me to a real sense of how I must act with You and others.*

dew

May God give you heaven's dew and earth's richness—an abundance of grain and new wine. —Genesis 27:28 (NIV)

G od kept bringing Bible passages about dew across my devotions. I wrote down several scriptures regarding dew and began praying through them. As a gardener, I was intrigued by its spiritual correlations and significance. Plants have dew on days when there is no rain. It saturates both flora and fauna with moisture needed for daily nourishment.

God similarly supplies our daily needs. I love the visual image of heavy, wet dewdrops resting on grass, leaves, and flowers. I pray that God will saturate me with what I need for today and that His goodness will rest upon me like the morning dew. I imagine God's provision, day after day, meeting me in the mornings as He does for creation.

—Brenda L. Yoder

Lord, allow Your dew to fall upon me,
saturating me with heaven's riches.

rend

Rend your heart and not your garments.
—Joel 2:13 (NIV)

R end" is not a word I usually use. The Merriam-Webster dictionary defines it as "to tear (the hair or clothing) as a sign of anger, grief or despair." I don't think I've ever ripped a piece of paper—let alone my clothing—as an out-pouring of grief. But I've learned that rending my heart is a necessary spiritual process, particularly when sin has crept in.

It can be all too easy to shy away from this task and to avoid looking at my sin at all by making excuses or allowing myself to be distracted. But that only contributes to sin's festering.

Consequently, when I sense a sin being pointed out in my life, I find myself praying this word over myself: "Rend. Rend my heart." This rending forces me to look squarely, steadily at these sins. Only then can I see them for what they are, and then repent and return to God with *all* my heart.

—Elizabeth James

Lord, help me look squarely at my sins and then rend my heart over them. Thank You that You abound in love and are always gracious to forgive. Amen.

ashes

To console those who mourn in Zion, to give them beauty for ashes . . . that He may be glorified. —Isaiah 61:3 (NKJV)

A few years ago, a major wildfire was stopped just a few miles from our home. Thankful to be safe when the fire was finally contained, I learned more than five hundred homes had been destroyed. Needless to say, our air quality was very poor, with smoke and ashes floating around us like snowflakes. When I stepped outside, the ashes spoke of destruction and disaster. But over time, the wind blew the ashes away.

The prophet Isaiah, a messenger for God, preached to the people of Judah. He unfolded future blessings through the Messiah. Instead of destruction and disaster, Jesus would bring restoration and new life and exchange ashes for beauty.

With our own personal fiery sins, how comforting it is that we don't remain in a state of disaster. Our Savior has come to deliver us. Christ gently blows the ashes away.

—Becky Van Vleet

Dear Lord, we praise Your name when You blow our ashes away and restore beauty in our souls.

timeless

Jesus doesn't change—yesterday, today, tomorrow,
he's always totally himself. —Hebrews 13:8 (MSG)

My friend Kathy asked me about my stress level, which often affects my health. My stress levels rose just thinking about my writing deadlines, my kids' and grandkids' messy lives, and my elderly Mom's health.

Then a truth interrupted that thought: Because God is timeless, He's already devised a plan to fix every problem that threatens to weigh me down. Every time I pray, Jesus doesn't wring His hands and turn to God and say, "What shall we do? This has never come up before!" No. He stands in front of me with a gracious smile and opens His hands wide to receive my cares.

Ahhh . . . I feel better now. Knowing human time and my limited perspective do not limit God, I gladly give Him my cares.

—Jeanette Levellie

*Dear God, thank You that because You are timeless,
You already know every good plan You created for
my family and me. I trust Your love. Amen.*

alone

But Jesus often withdrew to lonely places
and prayed. —Luke 5:16 (NIV)

The word *alone* can mean different things to different people—isolation and depression to one, rest and renewal to someone else. Sometimes I feel as though nothing good can come from being alone. The walls close in, the room grows dim, and suddenly the world has only one soul left in it. Me.

Then I remember that even Jesus purposefully went to be alone. It was a time of quiet reflection, intense worship, and powerful prayer. Away from the din of humanity, it was a sweet and intimate time with his heavenly Father in a place where he could focus all of his attention without distraction. Now when I'm alone, I relax into the moment and enjoy the relationship I have with the One who loves to be alone with me.

—Kimberly Shumate

Lord, bring me to that place of holy aloneness where
we can share peaceful communion together. Amen.

ephphatha

Then he looked up to heaven and groaned, and said to him, "*Ephphatha!*" (that is, "Be opened!") —Mark 7:34 (NABRE)

Push down and turn," the lid reads. Easy enough, right? I follow the instructions, but the lid doesn't yield to my aging hands. *Why are things so hard to open?* I think. "*Ephphatha,*" I say, pleading for divine intervention. Jesus prayed this word and opened the deaf man's ears. I know He will help me directly or provide the help of my husband's hand.

Something that's more difficult to open: hearts closed by prejudice and indifference. A grip so tight that we fail to recognize the needs of others and to share the gift of God's love.

When we struggle to open containers, we can find direction in the popular mnemonic "righty-tighty, lefty-loosey." When we struggle to open our hearts, we can find direction in His teachings and love.

—Mary Bredel Fike

*Ephphatha, Lord, we pray. Open
our hearts . . . and those tight lids!*

covet

There are those who covet greedily all day long; but the righteous give and don't withhold. —Proverbs 21:26 (WEB)

watched a lone seagull plunge into the Gulf, grab a small fish, and fly to the beach to feast on it. Before it could eat its catch, a covetous seagull tried to snatch the fish for itself, even though there were plenty of other fish in the water for it to have its own. It wanted "that" particular fish. The gull with the fish flew away performing all kinds of aerial acrobatics trying to escape the covetous bird in hot pursuit until they were both out of sight.

Don't we often covet what our neighbors have—material possessions, relationships, personal or physical characteristics, talents? I want to value the gifts God has given me and use them for His glory. Covet and make use of each moment of life upon this earth. Most importantly, covet and hold dear the love and life sacrificed for me by His Son.

—Ronald F. Lazenby

Oh, Giving God! Help me to be content with what You have given me and not covet that of my neighbor. Help me to covet only those things pleasing to You. Amen.

lamp

At that time the kingdom of heaven will be like ten virgins who took their lamps and went out to meet the bridegroom. Five of them were foolish and five were wise. The foolish ones took their lamps but did not take any oil with them. —Matthew 25:1–3 (NIV)

You may remember that the wise virgins later refused to share their lamp oil with the foolish virgins. This used to seem rather mean and petty to me, and decidedly un-Christian to boot. I mean, aren't we supposed to share out of our abundance? As I've matured in faith, my understanding has changed.

I've invested my heart and time over many years to embrace the light of Christ. This labor of love has been at times arduous, sacrificial, and even painful, though deeply rewarding.

I cannot just hand this to anyone. I can share the fruits of it, but the lamp oil was bought at a price, and someone who wants the reward must do the work for themselves. We each have to choose to be ready for the bridegroom.

—Isabella Campolattaro

Lord Jesus, may I gather and treasure the grace
of abundant oil for Your return.

vivid

You make known to me the path of life; in your presence there is fullness of joy . . . —Psalm 16:11 (ESV)

The riotous colors of my pansies welcome me home every day. Their bright, happy faces turn toward the sun while their roots soak up water.

I often wish my life could be as vivid as the purples and yellows displayed by my flowers. I tend to seek the next best thing—vacation, car, outfit—in my quest for a vivid life, one that will attract followers on social media.

But social media posts full of likes and follows hide an empty reality that is as fulfilling as forgetting to water my pansies and watching them fade to brown.

Should we strive to live our best lives, as the saying goes, in a material sense? No, we are to seek God's presence and there find the best spiritual life that God has for us. Just as pansies can't thrive solely by being in the sun, neither can we flourish and live vividly without God's Word. We need to soak our roots in Scripture.

—Bethany S. LaShell

Lord, help me remember to soak up the goodness of Your Word before seeking fulfillment in the world.

sing

The time to sing is when your emotional level is
just too high to speak anymore. —Bob Fosse

During my years of voice lessons, the hardest challenge
for me was how to push past the feeling of a lump in my
throat when a song made me emotional. All vocal control and technique would fly out the window as my eyes welled
up and my throat constricted. I learned that the secret to relaxing that panic response is just being within the song, whatever
emotions it stirs. Sometimes that's easier said than done!

There have certainly been times in my faith life where I felt
pressure to present a perfectly rehearsed and polished song
to my Lord. Shouldn't I know by now how to push past human
failings and minor hurts and sing flawlessly? But faith is not a
technique to be learned and performed. It is a living, breathing
thing that must be experienced as an integral part of all the
wild emotions life can bring. We can experience the beautiful
music as children of God—even if our voices wobble.

—Sarah Greek

I will sing of Your goodness through waves of emotions,
with squeaky notes and shaky breaths. Amen.

overwhelmed

When I am overwhelmed, you alone know the way
I should turn. —Psalm 142:3 (NLT)

Moving forty years of household contents is not a task for the faint of heart. My packed boxes were a fraction of what still remained in the master bedroom, den, and bookcases. I thought my sorting system of one pile to pack, one to donate, and one to discard would be efficient for my overwhelming project, but organization wasn't the problem. Energy and reminiscing were.

Discarding clothes that no longer fit or are in style is an easy decision. Sorting and reminiscing over scrapbooks, photo albums, and souvenirs is overwhelming. Memories flooded my heart and tears flowed. That's where I stopped packing and took a break.

That day, knowing the way I should turn didn't mean sorting piles for clothes and household contents. It was pausing to rest and gather energy to return later. It was also a time to remind myself that in my overwhelming moments, God would give me grace to do what He had called me to do—move.

—Marilyn Nutter

Father, help me to know which way to turn. Amen.

enable

So we keep praying for you, asking our God to enable you to live a life worthy of his call. —2 Thessalonians 1:11 (NLT)

One morning I found my daughter in her bedroom only partially dressed for school. She seemed frozen, with her head in a downcast tilt. When she noticed my presence, with my eyebrows lifted, her tears began to flow. "What if I do bad, Mom?" State-mandated standardized testing awaited her at school that morning. After some encouragement and a hug, she gathered herself together to start the day.

All morning, my mind refused to rest. I kept asking myself whether I should opt her out of the testing. The value of the assessment hardly seemed worth my daughter's anxiety over it. Yet I knew I wouldn't always be able to opt her out of the hard things of life. Both of us needed to learn to trust God to enable us to overcome our worry and fears. And at the end of four days of testing, she felt a sense of accomplishment, knowing that God had carried her through it.

—Becky Hofstad

Lord, enable us by Your power to release worry. Amen.

king

For the LORD Most High is awesome, the great King
over all the earth. —Psalm 47:2 (NIV)

Though I've typically worshipped and served in informal church settings, I've also been blessed by worship elsewhere, and I appreciate "high church" liturgy and practice. In my regular church practice, I kneel or bow with much less frequency than many of my Christian brothers and sisters. So, I've carried a practice into my "contemporary" worship life: Whenever a reading or song mentions God my King, I bow. If I'm seated, it may be just a nod. If I'm standing, I bow from the waist.

I don't speak, read, or hear the word *king* as much in my weekday life. But it's become a habit—a prayer to "the LORD Most High . . . the great King over all the earth." Like Abraham, Moses, Isaiah, and others, it's my joy to bow as a way of honoring Him and His presence in my life.

—Bob Hostetler

Lord, as the psalmist sang, I, by Your great love, can come into Your house; in reverence I bow down. Amen.

elevate

If one part suffers, every part suffers with it;
if one part is honored, every part rejoices with it.
—1 Corinthians 12:26 (NIV)

One week in Bible study with my third-grade girls' group, I realized only a few voices ever spoke up. Evangeline always had the correct answers. Alyson always had the funny quips. Dana always offered to read. But there were nearly a dozen other girls who sat, listening intently but never participating.

One week, I gathered my vocalizing rock stars and said, "How do you guys think we can get everyone to participate more?"

The next week, we launched Operation Elevate. *Who will open us in prayer? Who wants to put the felt figures on the board?* Using ideas from my tiny team, we watched as our shyest buddies started to shine.

After a few weeks, the girls all began to speak up. Taking the time to elevate one another's voices allowed us all to learn from one another.

—Ashley Kappel

Lord, help me to hold my tongue long enough to listen to those around me. Give them the confidence to share their learnings with me.

beauty

. . . this only do I seek: that I may dwell in the house of the LORD all the days of my life, to gaze on the beauty of the LORD and to seek him in his temple. —Psalm 27:4 (NIV)

Nine ancient rosebushes grace the front edge of my yard. I call them ancient because they were fully established and covered with thorns when we moved in over thirty years ago. They are still going strong.

It is my job to cut the spent blooms off the roses every few days throughout the summer. Often I find myself fretting over the spots on the leaves, which I can never get rid of. Yet passers-by on our quiet lane seem to notice only the beauty of roses blooming yellow, pink, and white. The compliments bestowed on my roses remind me to pray for eyes that focus on the beauty God has established in all of creation.

Beauty abounds. Even in the cross, as horrific as it was, there is beauty. When we look beyond the spotted leaves to focus on the roses, we get a glimpse of God.

—Linda L. Kruschke

Lord, open my eyes to see Your beauty in creation and in Your beloved children. Amen.

burden

Cast your burden on the LORD, and He shall sustain you.
—Psalm 55:22 (NKJV)

A burden is something we carry—like an awkwardly shaped bundle that keeps shifting. Burdens usually are physical, heavy, needed somewhere. But sometimes they weigh us down and tip us over at inconvenient moments.

When they slip from our arms or back, things we think important can break.

Sometimes it's our heart.

When we pray about a burden, we share the heavy load with the God who sees and knows how much we actually can carry.

Prayer allows us to ask for help to carry our loads more efficiently, or hand them off to the One who created us in the first place.

He'll remove burdens we didn't need to carry in the first place, and He'll help and encourage us through the ones we must endure ourselves.

—Michelle Ule

Thank You, Father, that You miss nothing and want to share our burdens.

commence

It is not your responsibility to finish the work, but neither are you free to desist from it. —Rabbi Tarfon

O nce there was a day in the office when I started a task first thing in the morning—and then it got interrupted almost immediately by a second task, which in turn was soon interrupted by a third. By the end of the day, I was eight tasks deep, and not a single one had been finished yet.

That was the day it became clear to me that in my life, I would commence a whole lot more than I would ever finish and be able to call an accomplishment. For a time, that made me reluctant to take on anything I thought was important to someone else or to the world at large. I didn't want to let anyone else down. Then slowly, it occurred to me that if a task was that vital, to commence it was enough. Even if I wasn't able to finish, someone else would take it up once it was begun.

—Rhoda Blecker

Thank You for showing me the importance of starting needful tasks—and trusting You to guide them to completion.

editor

You saw me before I was born. Every day of my life was recorded in your book. —Psalm 139:16 (NLT)

O f all the hats I wear, one I especially detest is the role of "editor." Much of my editing happens in manuscripts written by people under twenty. How does one go about editing the work of a budding sixteen-year-old writer without breaking the teen's creative spirit? I've spent thirty years trying to figure that out.

Maybe the origin of my hatred lies deep inside, with my "internal editor." In workshops, the leaders tell us to ignore that irritating voice inside that says *those sentences don't go together, that idea's ridiculous, that dialogue's stilted.* My internal editor works overtime, jumping from *you can't write* to *you're no good.* Then, I not only shut down the computer, but I fall into the traps of insecurity and despair.

Thankfully, my Real Editor steps in, takes me by my hand, shows me in His Word—His Perfectly Edited Word—how He wrote my story without a single mistake.

—Cathy Mayfield

Master Editor, thank You for my story, including Your saving grace.

biscuit

Your word is a lamp for my feet, a light on my path.
—Psalm 119:105 (NIV)

Is there a single word that tells the story of your life? Mine is *biscuit*.

I knew every multiple-syllable word in the *Words of the Champions* booklet. The one that was supposed to prepare me for the spelling bee that would win Mom and me a trip to see the cherry blossoms in our nation's capital. When they gave me the simple word *biscuit*, the world stood still. *Was it i before u or u before i?* Before the buzzer went off, I saw the blue-and-yellow box on our kitchen counter in my mind. "Bisquick!" I blurted to a snickering crowd.

Mom used the disappointment to teach me the best words of all. *Hope. Joy. Jesus. Yes.* Eventually, I did get to see those cherry blossoms. And by the time I traveled to Washington, DC, I knew that the words we live by are more important than the words we spell.

—Roberta Messner

Thank You for Your wonderful words of life, Lord.
And for always keeping Your word!

qāvâ

But those who wait on the Lord shall renew their strength.
—Isaiah 40:31 (NKJV)

I scan the forest floor looking for purple blossoms. The drab winter ground has been brown and lacking in life for months. Every year, fuzzy pasqueflowers offer the first whispers of spring. "Pasque" means "Passover," and these signature spring blooms always emerge during the Passover season. I eagerly anticipate their arrival and proclamation: new life is here!

The feeling reminds me of qāvâ, a Hebrew word that means to watch patiently, waiting with expectancy. The word is used in the verse quoted above, Isaiah 40:31—the word translated *wait*. It speaks not of a wishful, "hope for" waiting, but blessed assurance of what will surely come.

"Look there!" My husband directs my attention to a cluster of pasqueflowers on the hillside. Soon, we begin seeing them everywhere—more than we've ever seen in one area! They carpet the forest in color and hope. They are always worth the wait.

—Eryn Lynum

Dear Lord, help me to qāvâ—to wait in eager expectation and assurance of all You want to do in my life. Amen.

nudge

Listen for God's voice in everything you do, everywhere you go; he's the one who will keep you on track.
—Proverbs 3:6 (MSG)

M y husband and I were enjoying the coolness of the car air conditioner on a summer day. We passed a woman walking on the side of the road.

God nudged my husband and me at the same time to go back and ask the woman if she would like a ride.

My husband drove back to where the woman had paused to stand still in the shade. Not wanting to startle her, we slowly approached and lowered the window.

"Hello, ma'am, would you like a ride somewhere? You are welcome to ride with us."

"Thank you. It's so hot today. I would appreciate a ride and a chance to cool off."

We were thankful to have helped a stranger have relief from the heat and humidity—and for nudges from God.

—Melissa Henderson

Father, thank You for the nudges You give. Amen.

effortless

I will give you what you have not asked for.
—1 Kings 3:13 (NIV)

My friend told me that she loved seeing her daughter play the piano effortlessly. God picked up the word *effortless* and dropped it into my soul. I was in a season of professional and personal exhaustion. I longed for the experience of doing something effortlessly.

I started praying that God would create experiences in my life that were effortless—not that they would be without engagement or intention, but that they would be life-giving, not exhausting. *Effortless* became my prayer word for that year.

I let go of certain commitments while taking on new ones that embodied my word for the year. In one instance, God provided a job as a school counselor, which is second nature to me. Mental, emotional, and physical energy returned. God showed me that striving for things that were not within His plan drained me. Activities that aligned with His plans were effortless, and they brought joy and refreshing energy.

—Brenda Yoder

Lord, bring experiences in my life that are effortless and life-giving.

author

. . . looking unto Jesus, the author and finisher of our faith.
—Hebrews 12:2 (NKJV)

When I published my first book, the word *author* took on a deeper meaning. I realized that God has been writing my story from conception to death, giving me revelations of His greatness. It was astounding to think that every detail—every season and timing of events, every person who entered my story—has been thought out from beginning to end.

From my perspective, my life's story is written haphazardly. However, the Author has plotted each scene to be perfect for the ending. As Psalm 139:16 (NKJV) says, "Your eyes saw my substance, being yet unformed. And in Your book they all were written, the days fashioned for me, when as yet there were none of them."

As the Author and Finisher of my faith walk, God has written into my future the provisions, encounters, surprises, and hardships that will make my story perfect for me. He has an ending that will bring Him glory as I follow His story line.

—Betty A. Rodgers-Kulich

Lord, help me to remember that You are the Author and Finisher of my personal life story. You are taking care of all the details. Amen.

lift

And [Jesus] said: "Truly I tell you, unless you change
and become like little children, you will never enter the
kingdom of heaven." —Matthew 18:3 (NIV)

My little girl chatted across the counter with me after
her friend's father had died.

"Mom, everyone is saying that he's in heaven now
and that he got a hug from Jesus. When I see Jesus, I'm going
to ask Him for a piggyback ride!"

Her eyes glittered in expectation, as mine began to shimmer with the tears I was holding back. This must have been
what Jesus meant when He said that to enter His kingdom we
must come to Him like children. Full of expectation, running
into His arms to be joyfully thrown into the air.

I've seen my children come alive in this kind of love from
their father, but I've never dared to imagine asking Jesus for a
piggyback ride.

—Liz Ditty

*Father God, teach me what it feels like to be lifted up
by the strength of Your joy.*

dawn

Because of the tender mercy of our God, the dawn from on high will break upon us. —Luke 1:78 (NRSVUE)

———

"Come and look!" my husband called from the deck, pointing toward soft streaks of apricot and pink in the eastern sky. We both gazed silently and then turned slowly toward the west. There, the bright rays of morning sunlight touched the snow-covered Olympic Mountains, turning them the deepest rose-pink imaginable.

Dawn is a word of promise. For untold generations, God's people have risen at daybreak to open their hearts in prayer, receiving a fresh gift of tender mercy. Whatever shadow or darkness hovers near, the morning light dispels fear and illumines the path into a new day.

—Marlene Kropf

God of each new morning, let the dawn from on high renew us with Your mercy and guide our feet into the way of peace. Amen.

even

Though you have not seen him, you love him; and even though you do not see him now, you believe in him and are filled with an inexpressible and glorious joy.
—1 Peter 1:8 (NIV)

She lay sick in a hospital bed, while many around the world prayed for her complete healing, knowing our best power was prayer. Even though we didn't know if our prayers would make a difference. Even when we didn't know the outcome. Even if our friend never fully recovered. We knew our prayers brought us closer to Jesus.

Even so, even if, even though. I see these pairings and think of persistence through faith. Despite the circumstances, we believe we can make it through our struggles because God is with us, no matter what. Even when we don't know what to expect. Even if a situation doesn't go as planned. Even though we may not feel prepared for what's next. We believe in the power of Jesus's love for us.

—Susan Brehmer

Lord, I pray, even when it's hard. Even when I don't understand what's happening. May I have faith even then. Amen.

thrive

When the righteous thrive, the people rejoice.
—Proverbs 29:2 (NIV)

Our little bungalow faces south, with large windows allowing sunlight to pour into our living room all year round. My houseplants have thrived there despite my lack of green thumbs. Every other week I haul the plants to the kitchen sink, where I nearly drown them, then let them drain overnight. In the morning I return them to their sunny spots with an encouraging, "You're on your own 'til next time, kids. Now thrive!"

Except they're not on their own. I may provide them with water, but our Heavenly Father bestows them with what only He can give. I've been known to wander into that sunny space myself, simply to soak in the warmth and light. I stand tall, raise my arms, meditate on God's character, and remind myself I can thrive because He's provided everything I need.

—Terrie Todd

*God, teach me to soak in Your Word and Your promises
like the sunlight my plants and I need to thrive. Amen.*

encircled

You have encircled me behind and in front, and placed
Your hand upon me. —Psalm 139:5 (NASB)

A few days after receiving a cancer diagnosis, I was looking through my jewelry case and came upon a bracelet I had not worn in many years. It had several links
imprinted with words I needed to wear, not just on my wrist, but
also in my heart: *hope, trust, love, joy, family, courage.*

Each time my gaze would fall upon one of those links, my
mind was drawn to Scripture, which sustained and supported me
through the journey. My Lord and Healer was never far from me
during that time—just as He is always with me, even now that it
is past.

—Liz Kimmel

*Father, let me never forget that You have encircled
me with Your love and protection, no matter what
circumstances my life encounters. Amen.*

incense

Let my prayer be counted as incense before you, and
the lifting up of my hands as the evening sacrifice!
—Psalm 141:2 (ESV)

I love the smell of incense burning. I don't use it often, but
when I do, I'm reminded of my trips to the Middle East,
where I encountered it in the marketplace. Scripture reveals
that our heavenly Father likes it, too, but there is something He
desires even more—the praise of His people.

The psalmist, David, knew this. He longed for his worship to
be like a pleasant aroma in the nostrils of God. In other places
in the Bible, we read that incense was often used in a sacrifice
to God. The three wise men even brought frankincense as a gift
to worship the young Jesus.

Today there are many ways we may present pleasing offerings
to the Lord. We extend our talents, our money, our possessions—
we devote our entire lives wholly to Him. I believe that our
devotion and praise is like a beautiful fragrance to Him.

—Tez Brooks

*Father, like incense, may my walk with You forever be a
sweet-smelling aroma to Your nose. Amen.*

prophecy

The vision is yet for an appointed time . . . though it tarry,
wait for it. —Habakkuk 2:3 (KJV)

'm God's brat. When things don't go my way, I throw a tantrum.

"I want you to adopt," said the Voice. I obey. Sadly, the adoption falls through.

"You lied, Lord!" Lifting my finger to heaven, not fearing lightning, I address the Almighty. "I'll give you one more chance!"

I open my Bible, pointing blindly to the prophet Habakkuk. "The vision . . . tarry . . . wait." God's promise.

Awe. Tears. Forgiveness.

Years later, to join our family of eight, a phone call: two brothers. Two more phone calls added two teens to my growing family, a boy and a girl.

Then, the Voice: "I want you to adopt."

"I'm eighty!"

Habakkuk. Prophecy. A delightful teenage girl waits for me in Bulgaria.

—Mayra Fernandez

Lord, thank You for trusting me, Your beloved brat,
with these, Your children.

answer

Ask, and it shall be given you. —Matthew 7:7 (KJV)

Given my attention to detail, handling the family's finances was right up my alley. I wrote the check for our mortgage payment to coincide with a paycheck, setting aside the envelope containing the check for mailing closer to the due date.

One month the envelope with the mortgage payment was nowhere to be found when it came time for mailing. At my wit's end, I prayed as I drove to work one morning. *God, please let me find the envelope.* No sooner had this request been made than a car cut me off. My slamming on the brakes catapulted everything I'd placed on the passenger seat to the floor.

What? The missing envelope lay on the floor below the passenger seat; I'd tucked it into a book I was reading and forgotten it. The jolt had dislodged the envelope. God provided a quick answer in an unexpected way.

—Alice H. Murray

Dear God, open my eyes to see the ways You answer my prayers, since the means You use to do so are not always what I am anticipating. Amen.

spring

Truth shall spring out of the earth, and righteousness shall look down from heaven. —Psalm 85:11 (NKJV)

When my husband and I visited Steamboat Springs in northern Colorado with some friends, we heard about a walking tour of all the natural springs located in the town. We got the directions and began our trek, eager to see each one. Much to our amazement, each spring was unique. The bubbles and foam from these natural water wonders never stopped flowing.

The author of Psalm 85, one of Korah's sons, wrote a beautiful metaphor of truth springing up out of the earth. What a resplendent picture we have, that no matter the sin and destruction we deal with, God's truth will spring up around us, prevailing over our human tendencies.

Just as God's water springs out of the earth, we can cultivate His truth to spring out of our hearts. If we never allow it to stop flowing, righteousness shall look down upon us from heaven.

—Becky Van Vleet

O Lord, we thank You for Your truth. May it always spring from our hearts each day as we serve You.

sparkle

Don't allow a negative point of view to dull your sparkle and your love of life. —Lisa J. Morris

When I declutter, I often toss items in unlikely places, intending to put them in their rightful spot. Someday. Two weeks ago I threw some sparkly gold balloon weights on an end table next to my "prayer chair." That night I noticed my cat Wally playing with something flashy. I laughed when I saw he'd discovered the balloon weights. *Aha*, I thought, *where I meet God is the perfect place for some sparkle!*

When I need wisdom, God's Word sparks new thoughts. If I'm depressed, the comforting voice of God's Spirit sparks hope in my heart. When my praise seems dull and lifeless, God receives it as if a million fireworks lit the sky. And the best part? After I leave this place of prayer, I take His sparkle with me.

—Jeanette Levellie

Lord, thank You for the light of Your presence. May I sparkle today, to attract those in darkness to You. Amen.

pursue

Pursue peace with all people, and holiness, without which no one will see the Lord. —Hebrews 12:14 (NKJV)

I get along with everyone . . . until I don't.

Pursuing peace with people who honk their horns, wave their signs, or shout from the sidelines seems impossible. Pursuing peace with people who are rude, impatient, or unkind feels unthinkable. Pursuing peace with people with different beliefs, standards, or values seems inconceivable.

My heart's desire is for others to see Christ in me, but I can't pursue peace in the weakness of my flesh. I need the strength of Christ, the power of His Holy Spirit operating in and through me.

Before a sharp reply can form, I pray, *pursue*. When I'd rather lunge than love, I ask for grace to pursue a better answer. When I reach the end of me, a simple prayer rises within me: *Pursue*.

Pursue peace that Christ may be seen in me.

—Crystal Storms

Jesus, guard my tongue and overflow me with Your love. Give me grace to pursue peace that others may see You. Amen.

no

They will lift you up in their hands, so that you will not strike your foot against a stone. —Psalm 91:12 (NIV)

Like powdered sugar dusting the ground, the icy road snaked through the rural farmland between Eugene and Junction City. Oregon's Willamette Valley is a beautiful place, and my mind always wanders back to what the settlers must have thought as they crested the Cascade Mountains for their first look. But today was less eventful than the pioneers' journey, just a monthly ladies' luncheon.

Drivers notoriously ignored the conservative speed limit on these back roads. I took each curve slowly as I whispered Psalm 91. As I spoke the words, "No harm will overtake you, no disaster will come near your tent," a car flew around the bend, sliding sideways into my lane. As it headed directly at me, it came within inches before it careened into a tree.

The driver was okay. I was shaken. God was not.

—Kimberly Shumate

Lord of the past, present, and future, I pray that no harm coming in my direction will prevail.

spice

Spice a dish with love and it pleases every palate.
—attributed to Plautus

Imagine walking into an old-fashioned bakery. As you open the door, the warmth and scent of cinnamon rolls and creamy vanilla glaze envelop you with a spicy welcome. The enticing cocoa-rich brownies invite you to linger longer for an olfactory delight. Those sweet and spicy aromas can lift your spirits.

When we get caught up in our habits and day-to-day routine, we can become dispirited, failing to appreciate or even notice God's gifts around us. Our life's palate can become bland, taking on a "salt and pepper" taste. That's when we need to "stop and smell the roses" . . . or some cinnamon rolls.

Spice things up! Reconnect with God, family, and friends. Explore a different route to work. Engage in a new activity. Volunteer. You will soon discover the fact that variety *is* the spice of life.

—Mary Bredel Fike

Lord, help me to add some spice to my day and to season everything with love.

aware

When Jacob awoke from his sleep, he thought,
"Surely the LORD is in this place, and I was not aware of it."
—Genesis 28:16 (NIV)

The night I saw smoke pouring from under my hood was one of the scariest nights of my life. Visions of fiery explosions flashed before my eyes as I drove the car onto the shoulder of the interstate. Almost immediately, a kind trucker pulled in behind me to assist. He'd spotted the smoke before I had, and, unbeknownst to me, waited for me to pull off.

The patriarch Jacob had a Protector greater than my trucker friend, and Jacob was also unaware of His presence. The darkness of his circumstances made it hard to see Him. I'm learning, when I face scary situations, to ask God to make me aware of His presence. Although I can't see Him with my eyes, as Jacob did, I can see evidence of His love and care all around me.

—Lori Hatcher

Lord, make me aware of Your presence every day. Open my eyes that I might see Your protection and provision in my life.

bride

Let us rejoice and exult and give him the glory, for the marriage of the Lamb has come, and his Bride has made herself ready . . . —Revelation 19:7 (ESV)

The average cost of a wedding in 2021 was a whopping $28,000, while the average wedding dress cost more than $2,400! Even though I love a good party and a pretty dress more than average, I find those figures alarming. More so when you can consider that nearly 50 percent of American marriages fail by year nine.

The numbers nerd in me wants to check the correlation between expensive weddings and divorce. Are people who spend a lot on their ceremonies more likely to get divorced? More importantly, could it be that our priorities are just a little bit off?

I am deeply heartened by this verse in Revelation that blesses me with the ultimate wedding attire—"fine linen, bright and pure"—granted me by my heavenly bridegroom, Jesus Christ, free of charge. This holy marriage will last eternally, paid for entirely by the Lamb of God who took away my sin and will love me forever.

—Isabella Campolattaro

Lord Jesus, thank You for making me Your forever beloved bride!

groom

I am jealous for you with a godly jealousy. I promised you to one husband, to Christ, so that I might present you as a pure virgin to him. —2 Corinthians 11:2 (NIV)

Paul is speaking to the wayward Corinthians, who were positively off the rails with all sorts of bad behavior, including rampant sexual immorality. I believe that unlike human jealousy, Paul's jealousy—a reflection of God's—is motivated by pure spiritual love.

Paul knows that anything, *anything*, that diverts us from a wholehearted focus on Christ will harm us and prevent us from enjoying the full benefits of our spiritual "marriage" to the perfect husband.

Jesus is called our bridegroom repeatedly in Scripture because He fulfills all the most precious attributes we might long for in a husband: love, sacred passion, protection, and endless support. In seeking and receiving all this from our heavenly groom, we bless our "jealous" God with our faithfulness, even as we receive His blessing.

—Isabella Campolattaro

Jesus, may You ever remain my one true love.

home

Even the sparrow has found a home, and the swallow a nest for herself, where she may have her young—a place near your altar, LORD Almighty, my King and my God. —Psalm 84:3 (NIV)

My grandmother on my father's side lived on the same country road for ninety years. She mowed the same plot of ground, walked down the hill to the same creek, and lived in the same house she helped to build with her own two hands—for a lifetime. Home.

My other grandmother, on my mother's side, left her country road of sixty years and moved away. She left all she knew to be near my family after my grandfather died. She occupied a new house, made new friends, and attended a different church. Home.

I've pondered which of my grandmothers had the ideal situation. Both. I realize we all long to feel at home wherever we settle. To belong. If God makes sure that not only grandmothers but even sparrows are taken care of, I can trust Him to provide a home for me, both now and on that day when He comes to take me to live with Him. Home.

—April Strauch

Lord, thank You for the promise of Home. Amen.

shut

The animals going in were male and female of every living thing, as God had commanded Noah. Then the LORD shut him in. —Genesis 7:16 (NIV)

Our lives are full of so many paths, options, or choices. Social media can be overwhelming—but it can also steal untold amounts of our time. A few years ago, when visiting my daughter and her family, I didn't notice how inattentive I'd become until she asked me what was so important on my phone. At that time I had to humbly admit that I was addicted to my smartphone, and I asked God for help.

God wants us to be able to focus our lives on Him and Him alone. When I start feeling overwhelmed or distracted, I ask the Lord to *shut* me in so I can focus on Him. I ask him to *shut* out things that distract and keep me from focusing on Him, to *shut* out anything that may seek to harm me, to *shut* out the lies that make their way into my mind, to *shut* down my thoughts when they are not His thoughts.

—Jan Griffin

Lord, I pray that You will shut in the things You want to be a part of me and shut out things that take my focus off You.

propagate

For you have been born again, not of perishable seed,
but of imperishable, through the living and enduring
word of God. —1 Peter 1:23 (NIV)

My spirit wilts at the sight of spindly stems and shriveled leaves on my copper pinwheel plant. It was a gift from a friend and is my oldest living houseplant. It has traveled across states with my family and sat on the windowsill of four different homes.

Hesitantly holding its withered remains above the garbage can, I spot one tiny sprout. For a succulent, any hint of life means hope. Carefully, I remove the still-living leaf from the pot and tuck its roots into new soil.

It propagates fresh sprouts over the following months, overwhelming the little pot with new life. Its tender leaves are a tribute to a God who takes tiny hints of hope and propagates them into abundant life.

—Eryn Lynum

Dear Lord, restore the withered parts of my spirit.
Propagate new hope and life in my soul! Amen.

pattern

Do not conform to the pattern of this world, but
be transformed by the renewing of your mind.
—Romans 12:2 (NIV)

M y granddaughter Elliott burst with excitement over learning how to sew. We shopped for fabric and selected an easy pattern for a jumper. Once home, we opened the pattern envelope, carefully unfolding the delicate tissue.

"*This* is going to be a jumper?"

"Yes. We need to figure out which pieces we need, then we'll lay the paper on the fabric in a particular way, cut, and sew."

Elliott learned sewing was a process that took thought and time. Once we ironed the garment, she modeled her creation for the family. She looked beautiful.

Romans 12:2 reminds us to follow God's patterns for living: praying and seeing what the Bible offers us for wisdom and direction. When we thoughtfully follow God's plans and instructions, we model godly living—and that makes us look beautiful too.

—Marilyn Nutter

*Father, help me to go to Your Word for guidance
and to follow Your patterns. Amen.*

perspective

Be humble, thinking of others as better than yourselves.
—Philippians 2:3 (NLT)

A teenage girl and her mother trade jabs in heated arguments until each of them feels desperately misunderstood. The next day, they wake up to find they've traded bodies. This is the plot of *Freaky Friday*, a 2003 movie based on a book with the same title. My preteen daughters roared with laughter as the mother tried to play the guitar in her daughter's band. By the end of the movie, the characters had gained a new perspective on each other.

I wondered about inhabiting my daughters' bodies. What would it be like to be brown but have white parents? How would I feel walking around middle school with a less-than-smooth gait due to my disability? I found simply pondering life from their perspectives gives me insights that I might never have had otherwise. These insights help me to listen more and interject less, taking time to identify with what they are feeling.

—Becky Hofstad

Lord, please help me to make the effort to see things from the perspective of others and have a humble heart toward them. Amen.

garden

In simple humility, let our gardener, God, landscape you
with the Word, making a salvation-garden of your life.
—James 1:21 (MSG)

When my daughter Aubrey was in fifth grade, she and I planted a vegetable garden. Together we planned and plotted our tiny corner of the backyard, fenced it, turned the soil, planted seeds, watered, weeded, and awaited the harvest. I treasure memories of her sporting a prairie pioneer costume (from church dramas) while weeding. That year we enjoyed fresh lettuce, carrots, beans, cucumbers, and zucchini—lots of zucchini—from that little garden.

That memory informs my prayers to this day, as I ask God to thoroughly weed the garden of my heart, mind, and life, and cultivate a bumper crop of good things there: humility, wisdom, patience, love, joy, peace, and more. Sometimes, I pray it in a single word: *garden*.

—Bob Hostetler

*Yes, Lord, landscape me with Your Word, making a
salvation-garden of my life. Amen.*

bind

Be alert and of sober mind. Your enemy the devil prowls around like a roaring lion looking for someone to devour.
—1 Peter 5:8 (NIV)

Holidays can be hard; do you ever feel that way? I try not to get too caught up in the doing and going, but every year I find myself hitting a low during a big day.

Sometimes it comes because one of the kids is upset at something we did or did not do. Sometimes it's because the church service didn't go as smoothly as I'd hoped. Sometimes I'm just plain grumpy about something.

So this year, I decided to confront it head-on. *Lord,* I prayed, *please bless my preparations for Your holy days and bind the evil that tries to distract me from celebrating You.*

My holidays aren't magically easier. We still have tantrums, face disappointment, and get snippy, but I've found that my heart is lighter and my brain more capable of handling the obstacles as they arise.

—Ashley Kappel

Lord, in moments of celebrating You, bind Satan and all evil forces that would distract me from the true reason for the holidays.

willing

For no matter how many promises God has made,
they are "Yes" in Christ. —2 Corinthians 1:20 (NIV)

I agreed to join the leadership of a women's Bible study because I believed God had called me to that role. When I learned the weekly leaders' meeting was at 5:30 a.m. each Friday, I felt less willing. Nonetheless, I had made a commitment and I intended to keep it.

To say I'm not a morning person is an understatement. But I prayed God would help me rise at four o'clock to get to the meeting on time.

The first Friday, I awoke before my alarm and never hit the snooze button once. I arrived on time and full of joy every week. God rewarded my willingness to serve as a group leader with cherished friendships and a glimpse of His perfect faithfulness. He has grown my character, my leadership skills, and my relationship with Him, beyond anything I could have imagined. All because I was willing.

—Linda L. Kruschke

Lord, help me to always serve You with
a willing and joyful heart. Amen.

listening

The LORD came and stood there, calling as at the other times, "Samuel! Samuel!" Then Samuel said, "Speak, for your servant is listening." —1 Samuel 3:10 (NIV)

For a large part of my life, I didn't know that God was speaking to me. I started hearing His voice after I heard testimonies about the different ways He speaks to others.

I also found that when I ask Him questions, He answers. Sometimes it's an immediate response in my mind, through words, an inclination, or a picture.

One time I asked Him if there was anything, outside of the items on my packing list, I should bring on an upcoming mission trip to Mozambique. Dish gloves came to mind, so I packed them. After I arrived, I gave the gloves and a few other things to a missionary living on the base where we were staying. She said, "I've been wanting to buy dish gloves for the workers who wash our dishes, but I can't find any in stores!"

It's my delight to hear, listen, and follow His voice.

—Sarah Wind

Lord, speak to me. I am listening. Amen.

birds

The wind has painted fancies on my wings.
—Carmen Bernos de Gasztold

O ne of my roommates in Los Angeles was an artist. She worked in a lot of different media, and over the months we shared an apartment, I watched her create pictures in watercolor, tempera, oil, charcoal, and pencil. Every picture, no matter what the subject, whether it showed a view of inside, outside, or nothing identifiable, contained birds. I generally admired her work, but I was curious about the consistent presence of the birds. When I asked her why she always put a bird in a picture, she said that, to her, birds were the symbol of hope.

Now, every morning when I put out birdseed, my heart calls for birds to come and be nourished. Like my ex-roommate, I see them as symbols of hope, and I know God put them here on earth to inspire me to soar.

—Rhoda Blecker

God of the air, I can't help but envy Your birds. From their vantage point on high, they can see Your world without borders. Maybe that's why they sing.

courtesy

Do to others as you would like them to do to you.
—Luke 6:31 (NLT)

Navigating curvy roads at night requires high beams in the car. Courtesy reminds us to dim them when a car approaches from the opposite direction.

As our son-in-law drove me home late one night, his high beams lit the sides of the road as we both watched for the oft-crossing deer. He flicked the button to turn the bright lights down whenever a car came from ahead.

At one bend in the road, however, he turned his high beams off, though I didn't see a car coming. I wondered why he'd done so. Then I noticed the row of houses his lights would've intruded into had he not turned them off . . . the same houses I passed multiple times a month, never considering the people inside.

In one five-mile drive, my courteous son-in-law had taught me the true meaning of the Golden Rule.

—Cathy Mayfield

Jesus, whether in a car, our home, or a public place,
teach me to do to others as You would.

umbrella

When you pass through the waters, I will be with you.
—Isaiah 43:2 (NIV)

Like most folks, I've experienced my share of life's storms. Some, like starting over after a divorce in midlife, were bona fide gulley washers. I made it to the other side because of the One who speaks peace in the midst of the storm, who whispered it wouldn't last forever, and when it was over, I'd be stronger than ever.

If you were to peek at the passenger seat of my car during stormy weather, you'd see something that might make you scratch your head—a small stack of collapsible umbrellas with cards enclosed in tiny resealable plastic bags. My scribbles proclaim: "It won't rain always." Or "Every storm runs out of rain." Or my favorite: "Jesus is your shelter in your time of storm." When I spot someone in a downpour without an umbrella, it's my chance to pass along the great good news.

—Roberta Messner

Storm clouds may threaten, Lord, but we are ever in Your care.

nevertheless

Nevertheless he saved them for his name's sake,
that he might make his mighty power to be known.
—Psalm 106:8 (KJV)

At my appearance in traffic court, I noticed everyone pleaded not guilty. I saw that did not go well for them and decided I would plead guilty—adding I'd like to explain the circumstances.

The judge listened, then shook his head. "You're guilty." My heart sank, and tears rimmed my eyes. "Nevertheless," he added, "I'm going to dismiss the citation." I wiped my tears and left the courthouse with a sigh of relief. I was guilty, but not condemned.

I don't know why the judge let me go. I'm just glad he did. Whenever I recall that experience, it reminds me that I am also guilty of sin. But because of my love relationship with Christ and the blood sacrifice He made for me on the cross, I am assured of God's forgiveness. I'm guilty. Nevertheless, I'm not condemned.

—Penny L. Hunt

Father God, thank You for Your forgiveness and saving grace through Jesus Christ, our Lord.

rest

Come to Me, all you who labor and are heavy laden, and I will give you rest. —Matthew 11:28 (NKJV)

Hard days come in varying ways. Sickness that wears us out. Stress that wears on us. Struggles that wear us down. I long for relief on the hard days, but even when times are good, my heart cries: rest.

In both the good and the hard, I can rest in the truth that Jesus is with me. Rest in the knowledge I don't face the day alone or in my own strength. Rest in the sweetness of His presence.

In my weariness, I ask for His rest. When I am yoked with Jesus, He carries me through. With my gaze directed His way, He leads the way. I learn to walk in rhythm with the heartbeat of Christ. His pace allows for stillness and peace, and it makes space for loving others.

Rest allows me to find ease amid the hard days and gives me space to seek His guidance on the good. Rest brings me peace no matter the circumstances. Rest comes with the awareness of His presence.

—Crystal Storms

Jesus, thank You for the invitation to come to You and receive rest. Help me to walk yoked with You and to learn Your ways. Amen.

balance

To everything there is a season, a time for every purpose under heaven. —Ecclesiastes 3:1 (NKJV)

My husband and I love hiking through forests and along fast-flowing streams. The sounds and scents of nature bring us to life.

But a recent brain injury has left my husband's depth perception permanently damaged. When he climbs upward or descends a slope, he loses his balance. As a result, we now choose only level paths.

Entering this new season of life, I'm learning to appreciate these walks with my heart as well as my eyes and other senses. The sights we see are still pretty, and my spouse is safe. Our hikes are less about what we see and more about enjoying each other.

I'm gaining a better sense of balance in our marriage and in my relationship with God. As my reliance on Him deepens, the path He's chosen for me becomes clearer. My faith has found balance, for now and all seasons.

—Heidi Gaul

God, thank You for showing me balance and understanding for the beautiful seasons of life. Amen.

yell

This poor man cried out, and the Lord heard him, and saved him out of all his troubles. —Psalm 34:6 (NKJV)

There was a small grocery store I frequented when my daughter was young. They didn't have a big intercom system. If cashiers needed help bagging groceries, they would yell for help and the nearest bag boy would come running.

My child had seen this action displayed repeatedly.

On one particular occasion, she thought she'd preempt the cashier. She yelled, "SACK UP!" as loud as she could while I placed my items on the conveyor belt.

Then she excitedly watched for someone to answer that call.

God encourages us to yell (cry out) when we're in need, confused, broken, or lost. Yell when we're in trouble. Yell when we're distressed. He'll come running. Yell.

—Kristen West

Father, I lift up my voice and yell today—rescue me!

remnant

I will make the lame my remnant, those driven
away a strong nation. —Micah 4:7 (NIV)

Remnant. I didn't always think this was an important word. It's hard to believe a remnant—anything incomplete or less than perfect—has value. That changed when Micah 4 caught my eye.

I have cerebral palsy, so I qualify for the biblical adjective *lame*. Whether or not our culture does it intentionally, people like me can spend a large part of our lives feeling like outsiders, exiles with nowhere to belong.

It turns out that God has a much different view of remnants. He tends to pay them greater attention, deliberately collecting grieving, isolated people for purposes of His own. Not mockery, but unexpected transformation. In Him, we the lame discover He cherishes us. Joyous celebration and security overwhelm all that had been negative.

—Heidi Dru Kortman

Thank You, Lord, that we, who so often feel insignificant, can look forward to the day You come to rule and turn all our sorrows and frustrations into joy. Amen.

advocate

And I will ask the Father, and he will give you
another advocate to help you and be with you forever.
—John 14:16 (NIV)

For ten years I worked for an attorney whose job was, put simply, to advocate for his clients. He helped people reorganize their businesses, get the best custody arrangement for the sake of their children, and straighten out differences over property. While dealing with clients in crisis, I learned to listen, weigh my words, and advocate for them with the attorney, who happened to be my husband. We did our best to meet the needs of people in our small town.

When I pray, I have the comfort that the Holy Spirit advocates on my behalf with the heavenly Father. Knowing the Spirit dwells in me gives me assurance that He will know my concerns and needs even better than I do, and can petition more effectively than I could. Like the best lawyer in town, He seeks my best as my prayer case sits in the heavenly courtroom.

—Janet Holm McHenry

Thank You, God, that Your Spirit advocates on my behalf.

bends

Because he bends down to listen, I will pray
as long as I have breath! —Psalm 116:2 (NLT)

My son fell outside on the driveway and scraped up his hand. At the sound of his wailing, his sisters and I ran to his side. When the girls tried to convince him to let them see, he covered the scrape with his chubby fingers and pulled away with a teary scowl. He didn't trust them. He'd been the victim of their teasing one too many times.

But when I bent down with gentle words, he finally uncovered his injured hand to let me examine the damage. My posture invited trust and compassion. I closed the distance between us to wipe away the tears from his cheeks.

In that same way, Jesus closed the distance between heaven and earth to show us the depth of His love. He delights in His children, and He invites us to put our wounds before him so that He can make them better.

—Tara Johnson

Thank You, Lord, for being a good Father.
Remind me to bring all my hurts to You.

prune

He cuts off every branch in me that bears no fruit, while every branch that does bear fruit he prunes so that it will be even more fruitful. —John 15:2 (NIV)

Virginia creeper was slowly invading my cherished wisteria. No matter how often I pruned the intrusive plant, it seemed like a losing battle. As soon as I pruned one section, another plant would take its place.

How many times had I felt like that in my own life? How often had I tried to prune life's sorrows instead of allowing God to take hold of the shears? How many times had I relied on my own strength when I struggled with negative thoughts, or questioned whether God even heard my anguished prayers?

As I contemplated my own Virginia creeper, I remembered that I cannot get through life without the help of God. I needed to ask for His love to support me, to pray for help with one word: *prune*.

—Jeannie Hughes

Lord, please take control of my shears and help me prune out life's sorrows. Amen.

dwell

Let the word of Christ dwell in you richly, teaching and admonishing one another in all wisdom, singing psalms and hymns and spiritual songs, with thankfulness in your hearts to God. —Colossians 3:16 (ESV)

When the days turn warm and the light lasts long into the evening, I itch to bring out the grill. Nothing signals summer like the smoky scent of charcoal or the tanginess of grilled pineapple and slightly burnt hot dogs. But the best meal from the grill is the meat that's been marinated. Piercing the meat and letting it sit in a marinade hours before grilling enhances the flavors as they meld together and soak deep into the meat, ensuring a juicy and satisfying outcome.

Like the flavor of meat that grows deeper through marination, so our lives take on a rich quality when we let the word of Christ dwell in us. From faith-filled friends to worship songs to who we follow online, we can be people who invite Christ to dwell in us richly by ensuring His word saturates our days.

—Heather Kaufman

Lord, may the message of Christ dwell in me richly and transform me from the inside out. Amen.

refuge

I will say of the LORD, "He is my refuge and my fortress, my God, in whom I trust." —Psalm 91:2 (NIV)

A few years ago, a mama robin built a nest in the light fixture right by the front door. Every time we opened the front door, mama robin would get fussy. She had created a safe place for her babies. We tried not to bother her, but the robin didn't understand we were not a threat to the pale-blue eggs she was protecting.

We have a place of refuge as well. When troubles threaten to shake our world, as they most certainly will, we can rest assured that God is with us. He stands guard, ready to protect us. When challenges of this world become too much, we can run to God, hide under His wings, and rest safely in His care.

—Prasanta Verma

Dear God, thank You for being a place of refuge for us amid trials and difficulties. Amen.

ain't

And which of you by worrying can add one
cubit to his stature? —Luke 12:25 (NKJV)

My wife and I wrestled with the nine-foot Christmas tree we'd brought home from the lot, but there was no way it would fit through our front door. Our children were too young to help, but then we saw our neighbor Gene amble past on his afternoon stroll.

"Could you help us out here, Gene?" I asked.

He stopped in our driveway and assessed the situation. Finally, he said, "Ain't my tree," and kept walking.

I was dumbfounded, but then I realized he was right—our predicament wasn't his problem. We managed to drag the tree around the house and fit it through the sliding glass door in the back.

Since then, Gene's pronouncement has become a popular refrain in our family. Whenever there's a situation that isn't ours to worry about, we simply say, "Ain't my tree."

—Paul Elkins

Lord, help me to discern when it's the right time
to step in and help, or when it ain't my tree.

guidance

For this God is our God for ever and ever: he will be our guide even to the end. —Psalm 48:14 (NIV)

A group of my coworkers and I decided to share a ride to an off-site meeting in the company minivan. Before leaving the parking lot, we discovered that the removable back seat was not installed properly, so two of the men set to work putting it back where it belonged. They struggled unsuccessfully in the cold until finally the company technical writer reached into the van's glove compartment and pulled out the user's manual. Immediately after reading the two-sentence guidance on the seat's installation, the men slid and latched it right into place.

The written word is powerful. It can provide instruction, inspiration, and entertainment. But what about those things that don't come with directions, like marriage, parenting, and life in general? We have a user's manual for *all* those things: the Bible. When a question or dilemma arises, we need only consult it for guidance.

—Kim Sheard

Lord, thank You for providing us with the guidance of Your Word. Remind us to consult it often. Amen.

consider

Consider it pure joy, my brothers and sisters, whenever you face trials of many kinds. —James 1:2 (NIV)

It was raining and my tire was flat. Not only was I about to be soaking wet and dirty, but I also was going to miss an important meeting. I shook my head, mad at God. *Why, Lord? Why now?*

Burdens are never fun. Whether facing difficulties in relationships, our health, finances, persecution, or some other hardship, James reminds us to consider it differently—to be joyful. Easier said than done. We forget how a grateful heart in any situation pleases our Lord and transforms us.

Something important happens when we thank God for tribulations. A thankful heart changes our outlook on life. I want to learn to respond with, "This might be bad, but God will get me through it. I will be refined, stronger, and closer to God." Whether God delivers us from the fire or walks through it with us, remember that He never leaves us. For that, we can be joyful.

—Tez Brooks

Father, teach me to consider trials a blessing,
for they make me grow spiritually. Amen.

desire

Earth has nothing I desire besides you. —Psalm 73:25 (NIV)

M y brothers are five and nine years older than me, so having to wear their hand-me-downs as a boy ensured that I was never on the cutting edge of fashion. For a time, I desired nothing more fervently than a Nehru jacket, but by the time my parents gave in to my pleas, the fad had passed. The best I could do for school picture day was to wear a psychedelic kerchief around my neck . . . that clashed fantastically with my plaid shirt.

Desire can deceive—or delight. Eve's desire for the forbidden fruit proved disastrous (Genesis 3:6–21), while Paul's desire for the Philippians to bear spiritual fruit brought blessing (Philippians 4:15–17). A frequent prayer of mine is for God to fashion my desires until I want nothing on earth besides Him (Psalm 73:25). When my desires align with His will and ways, He will grant the desires of my heart (Psalm 37:4).

—Bob Hostetler

God, let my desires today align with Your will and ways. Amen.

neighbor

Let no one seek his own good, but the good of his neighbor.
—1 Corinthians 10:24 (ESV)

The Bible speaks of our neighbor, and we strive to recognize our "neighbor" in our daily lives. For my husband and me, a small change made a big difference in our perspective. For several years we tried to walk regularly at a nearby park that offers a lovely, forested path. However, about a year ago we decided to do our walk in our own neighborhood. Looking back, we now wonder why we used to drive to the park.

We live in North Africa where most people walk everywhere. Soon we found ourselves frequenting the vegetable cart of the man struggling economically, getting to know a woman selling embroidery on the street as we met her pregnant daughter, and responding cheerfully in English to teenagers trying out their limited language skills. By forsaking a crafted park pathway to follow the noise and life of our neighborhood, we discovered so many opportunities to seek ways to be good to our neighbors.

—Connie McDaniel

Dear Lord, lead me to my neighbors in my daily life. Allow me to really see them and to do good for them. Amen.

sustain

Cast your cares on the LORD and he will sustain you; he will never let the righteous be shaken. —Psalm 55:22 (NIV)

A fter a period of physical inactivity in my life, a friend invited me to a fitness class at the local YMCA. I agreed, thinking my body couldn't be *that* out of shape. As the music started and we began, I soon realized there was no way I would be able to sustain that level of intensity for the duration of the class.

Sometimes life can feel like a high-impact workout that we are tackling with an out-of-shape body. We lack what is needed to keep going. In these moments, Scripture invites us to cast all our cares on our loving Savior, who promises that He will sustain us. He will provide us the physical, mental, and emotional support that we need, enabling us to take the next step of our journey.

—Mindy Baker

Lord, I cast all my cares on You. Sustain me along life's difficult journey. Keep me from falling.

all

He is before all things, and by him all things hold together.
—Colossians 1:17 (CSB)

One of the most significant differences between living in the city and the country is the stars. One night shortly after moving to the country, I sat outside and embraced the splendor of the night. To my surprise, the longer I looked, the more the stars filled the black canvas. And the few stars that first caught my eye were now lost in the all-consuming light display before me.

In the same way, the more you look to Jesus, the more Jesus you will see. All things are held together by Him, and all things are relevant to Him. So, when I pray the word *all*, I look around the room, and remember: Jesus holds together every molecule of everything I see. Yet He is also all-devoted to us and is present for all that life is throwing at us now.

—AJ Smith

*Lord Jesus, help me to see You in all things
and trust You with all things.*

serene

If you look at the world you'll be distressed. If you look within, you'll be depressed. If you look at God, you'll be at rest.
—Corrie ten Boom

I sit and gaze at the five bird feeders swaying in the spring breeze from the eaves outside my dining room windows. A sense of serenity steals into my heart.

When my husband, Kevin, and I moved from LA to rural Illinois twenty-two years ago, we thought every moment would be like this. We'd sit in the backyard and sip iced tea, wave to neighbors, and thank the Lord for our slow, problem-free lives. Ha! We soon—in a couple of days—discovered that problems follow everyone, city folk and country folk alike.

We've learned to look at God for our serenity. Only He can give inner peace—the kind that lasts longer than a couple days.
—Jeanette Levellie

Dear God, I appreciate that no matter what happens around me—peace or chaos—You are always there for me with Your sweet serenity. Amen.

less

He must become greater; I must become less.
—John 3:30 (NIV)

For years I was a wannabe runner. A milestone birthday on the horizon convinced me it was now or never.

To keep from huffing and puffing my way through those first runs, I focused on breathing out, knowing my body would take in the oxygen it needed on its own. God spoke to my heart during one of those workouts: *This is how you magnify Me, how you live out less of you and more of Me.*

As I focus on the less, He increases. I breathe along with the mindfulness app on my watch a few times a day. With each breath, I'm reminded less of me, more of Him.

My prayer as I sit down to write: *less.* That Christ may be magnified through my words. My heart cry as I walk to the lectern to speak: *less.* That God may speak through me. My desire as I serve my family: *less.* That the love of Jesus may be shown through me.

—Crystal Storms

Jesus, less of me and more of You. More of Your peace. More of Your grace. More of Your presence. Amen.

reach

Your love, LORD, reaches to the heavens. —Psalm 36:5 (NIV)

J esus used everyday objects to teach important truths. One of my lessons came from a measuring tape—the carpenter's variety, where the tape is encased in a hard shell and can be stretched out and snatched back at the press of a button.

The measuring tape image was offered to me as a picture of my love. While it has the capacity to be far-reaching, it's also true that one little touch of the button can send it retreating, retracting, and recoiling inside its hard little shell.

When people push my button (*that* button), my love can go from reaching to retracting, moving farther away from them, and becoming all wrapped up in me. Suddenly, those who may need my love no longer have access to it. It is, quite literally, out of their reach.

God's love reaches; it doesn't retract. When we don't measure up, it reaches further still.

—Jenny Gehman

God of love, help me to reach and not retract. Amen.

ice cream

He asked for water, and she provided milk; she presented him cream in a majestic bowl. —Judges 5:25 (CEB)

What would you preach about?" I asked the seven-year-old in our morning Sunday school time. He had just made a negative remark about the pastor's sermon, so I informed him that he could preach next Sunday.

His response was, "ice cream." We then proceeded to discuss the ingredients of this delicious dish and if they were available during ancient biblical days. This sparked a new adventure into God's Word to find the animals that would provide milk or cream to make this treat.

"How would you use 'ice cream' in a sermon?" I asked. Without any thought he instantly responded, "God is better than ice cream!"

Jesus reminds us that we are to come to Him with the complete trust and openness of a child—to be able to share all our thoughts, ideas, goals, and even silly conversations over ice cream.

—Darci Werner

Lord, remind us that whenever life becomes too "adult"
that You are always better than ice cream.

sunlight

When Jesus spoke again to the people, he said, "I am the light of the world. Whoever follows me will never walk in darkness, but will have the light of life." —John 8:12 (NIV)

One summer, I visited Lisbon, Portugal, a city on seven hills. One site I visited was Our Lady of Mount Carmel, the ruins of a cathedral. On All Saints Day, November 1, 1755, an earthquake at about 9:40 a.m. caused the ceiling to collapse onto worshippers. I tried to imagine what must have been a chaotic scene when screams and dust filled that space. But the day I was there, this sanctuary was quiet, and sunlight streamed in through the vaulted arches that hung on blue sky.

I sat under those arches for a long time and thought about how the ceiling had been a physical barrier to the heavens, and how its removal resulted in this sunlight-filled space. I wondered what barriers I could bring down to better let in the Light.

—Nancy Schrock

Lord, help me to remove whatever barriers
keep me from You. Amen.

wake

The hour has already come for you to wake up from your slumber, because our salvation is nearer now than when we first believed. —Romans 13:11 (NIV)

The last few years have been extraordinarily challenging worldwide. We've lived through a pandemic, civil unrest, global conflict, increased violence, natural disasters, financial reversals, and all manner of other drama. All of these challenges are God-sized. We're still reeling and dealing with fallout of humanity's best thinking in trying to solve these dilemmas.

The term "woke" has powerful significance these days. However, I'd like to broaden the idea of being awake to capture the fullness Paul refers to here. It's past time that we waken from our spiritual slumber to realign ourselves with God and His word.

It's my heartfelt belief and firsthand experience that God wants to use all things to draw us ever closer to Himself. Let's awaken to God's call to enjoy His wisdom and protection anew.

—Isabella Campolattaro

Heavenly Father, help us respond to Your prompt to awaken to You and Your Truth.

carry

Carry each other's burdens, and in this way you will fulfill the law of Christ. —Galatians 6:2 (NIV)

D on't worry, Mommy, I can carry these. You don't have to," my daughter said to me as I lifted her out of her car seat. She was referring to her permanently attached "blankie" and three of her favorite "stuffies." As I carried her through the parking lot, I refrained from explaining to her that technically I was the one carrying them, since I was carrying *her* carrying them. I didn't want to squelch her sweet desire to help.

We carry many burdens in life. Sometimes it feels like too much. I was reminded that day that even when we feel like we are carrying a lot, God is the one doing the heavy lifting. He carries all of our burdens, because He carries us.

—Juliette Alvey

Lord, thank You for carrying me and every burden that I carry. Amen.

tap

Gentleness is strength under control. —Elizabeth George

I n my early days of learning to play pickleball, I focused on hitting the ball as hard as I could. I stood at the baseline and did my best to slam it cross-court over the net. I loved the satisfying *thwack* the ball made when I smacked it with my paddle. It went out of bounds more times than it stayed in, but I prided myself on my strong shots nonetheless.

It didn't take long, though, to notice what the more experienced players were doing. They often stood closer to the net—just outside the "kitchen line"—and gently tapped the ball over into just the right spot. Those who'd mastered that skill instead of muscling every shot almost always won the point.

It would seem that in pickleball and—more importantly—in life, the way we model the strength of Jesus is not by using brute force, but by using gentleness.

—Jennie Ivey

Tap me on the shoulder, dear Lord, and remind me to be gentle.

partake

Because there is one loaf, we, who are many, are one body, for we all share the one loaf. —1 Corinthians 10:17 (NIV)

When we moved outside the city's limits, my biggest concern was that our children would not have neighborhood buddies to play with. I prayed earnestly for good friends for them—for all of us.

A few weeks after our move, we sat around the table in one of our neighbors' homes. I had been nervous when they invited us to partake in their family Shabbat dinner because we were unfamiliar with the customs surrounding it, but my soul was refreshed by their hospitality.

They opened the evening with a Hebrew hymn. The words were foreign to me, but clearly their young children knew them and their meanings by heart. We then each shared a Scripture reading. Partaking together in the traditional Jewish challah bread and remembering God's provision of manna in the wilderness, I was overwhelmed with gratitude for His provision of fellowship in a new and unfamiliar place.

—Eryn Lynum

Dear Lord, help me to partake of Your every provision. Amen.

father

He got up, rebuked the wind and said to the waves, "Quiet! Be still!" Then the wind died down and it was completely calm. —Mark 4:39 (NIV)

I grew up in Guyana, South America, whose name means "land of many waters." I lived on the west coast and usually traveled by ferry across the river that separated my home from the city where I went to school. When I was about eight years old, my father suggested we cross the river by speedboat instead, to shorten the time of our commute.

I did not anticipate that the speedboat operator would have us sit at different places on the boat to keep the weight balanced. I remember feeling fear and anxiety as the boat left the shore and absolute terror as rough waves crashed against it.

The one thing that kept me from an absolute panic attack was the look of calm on my father's face. Even as the waves rolled in and the winds tossed the boat about, he remained composed. In all this, I kept my eyes fixed on my father.

—Stacy Pelotshweu

Heavenly Father, I will keep my eyes fixed on You because I know even the wind and the waves obey You. Amen.

try

Test me, LORD, and try me, examine my heart
and my mind. —Psalm 26:2 (NIV)

I grew up going to Sunday school every week. There, from early on, I learned this song verse (from Psalm 139):

Search me, O God, and know my heart today;
Try me, O Savior, know my thoughts, I pray.
See if there be some wicked way in me;
Cleanse me from ev'ry sin and set me free.*

I didn't know what it meant for God to "try" me; if I had known it meant "test me," I might have sung it less enthusiastically.

Years later I learned a different "try me" prayer that has been sung by many gospel singers—and has been a blessing to me when I've fallen down or failed in some way. It's a prayer of repentance. A prayer of recommitment. A prayer for starting over: "Try me one more time."

—Bob Hostetler

Lord, forgive me, and try me one more time. Amen.

---

*J. Edwin Orr, "Search Me, O God," public domain.

agape

. . . not giving up meeting together, as some are in the habit of doing, but encouraging one another.
—Hebrews 10:25 (NIV)

When I was in college, I joined our Christian fellowship group, Agape. It was there I met dozens of men and women who were dedicated to loving the Lord while also working to survive the demands of college classes and athletics.

Every Friday we met for an hour to worship Jesus, share our troubles, and listen to God's Word. Even though I grew up in a Christian school, I had never had such openness with what were essentially near perfect strangers.

It was in that group that I learned that *agape* can mean two things: the fatherly love of God, or a state of being wide open with wonder and surprise. And it was there that I experienced both completely. As I embraced, I too was embraced, and as a result, God cracked open my heart with such wonder and surprise that I truly learned how vast His love is for me, and for all those who love Him.

—Ashley Kappel

Lord, I pray that your followers find fellowship among believers that is teeming with agape love for You and for one another.

hineni

But the angel of the Lord called to him from heaven and said, "Abraham, Abraham!" And he said, "Here I am."
—Genesis 22:11 (ESV)

Sometimes God asks the impossible. Last summer God asked me to homeschool our kids. My husband didn't think it seemed wise. I knew it would stretch me in ways I wouldn't like and wasn't ready for. Doubts overwhelmed me. What if I wasn't enough? God's ask defied human logic, but what He wanted me to do was unmistakable.

So I answered, simply, "*Hineni.*" This word—the same one used in the verse above—is Hebrew for "here I am." I'm willing. All in. My answer is already yes to what You have prepared for me to do.

Then I waited and prayed. I prayed for the Lord to move my husband's heart. I prayed for guidance. That summer God cultivated a holy dependence in me. God provided everything I needed to go forward in obedience. This year has been messy and beautiful because I answered *hineni.*

—Amy Lindberg

Lord, hineni. Here I am. Use me for Your glory, in Your kingdom on earth, in whatever way You choose. Amen.

phila

Be devoted to one another in brotherly love; give preference to one another in honor. —Romans 12:10 (NASB)

The word *phila* in Greek refers to a close friend. This is the type of friendship seen between Jesus and His disciples, and God and Abraham. We are called to be *philas* to one another as the body of Christ. This kind of dedication to one another should be unmatched as we honor each other through self-sacrifice, offered through prayer, discipleship, or just lending a willing ear to listen, like Job's friends did.

I don't know what I would do without my *philas*. They are godly women who introduced me to Jesus. They lift me up in prayer, cry with me, laugh with me, challenge me, share the Word with me, and act as the hands and feet of Jesus when I need them. My life is changed because they chose to be devoted in brotherly love and gave preference to me, in honor.

—Dawn Marie Day

Lord, may I be devoted to my brothers and sisters in Christ, as You have called me to be. May I be an honoring phila *to them so they will know that they are dear, beloved, and cherished.*

path

Trust in the LORD with all your heart and lean not on your own understanding; in all your ways submit to him, and he will make your paths straight. —Proverbs 3:5–6 (NIV)

I stood at the bottom of the snowy hill. My granddaughter perched at the top on her new purple sled. "Watch out for the tree!" I called. She smiled and waved. As she pushed off, the sled gathered speed and then veered directly toward the tree. My granddaughter rolled off just before impact. "Why didn't you tell me to watch out for the tree?" she asked tearfully.

I often ask God for guidance. But I don't always listen. Like my granddaughter on that hill, sometimes I am too far away. Or maybe I'm distracted by the sparkling snow or the prospect of a thrilling ride before me.

My solution is to get closer to God. Pray. Read the Bible. Pay attention. When I keep my focus on God, I am better able to hear His direction. And that will always keep me gliding down the right path.

—Peggy Frezon

Lord, please grant me the boldness to ask You which path to take, the patience to wait for Your reply, and the wisdom to listen.

atonement

Our existence is an experiment. —Lawrence Kushner

Every year, in the week between Rosh Hashanah and Yom Kippur, I make atonement to a friend or family member for anything I might have said or done in the past year to hurt or offend them. I do it because Yom Kippur is a time to atone to God, and God will not let me atone that day unless I have already set things right with other human beings.

There is a third kind of atonement, but every year I have a lot of trouble with that one. I am also supposed to make atonement to myself for the ways I have hurt myself. Somehow, that's always harder. I find it easier to be "at one" with my friends and God than to be at one with myself. So as I pray the word *atonement*, I'll make it a reminder to be kind to myself too.

—Rhoda Blecker

Lord, You certainly knew what You were doing when You gave us a chance to make things right every single year. Every single year I need it!

block

The Holy Spirit will give you the right words when the time comes. —Luke 12:12 (MSG)

Ever heard of writer's block? A writer sits to create, turns to a blank page, picks up her pen. Which idea will she choose—that one she'd scribbled on the bottom of her Starbucks cup? Anticipation begins . . . then, wham! Like a toddler slamming a wooden block, every word returns to the dictionary from whence it came.

It reminds me of those times when I've chatted with people about something God did in my life. A nudge from the Holy Spirit urges me to boldly share the good news of Jesus's life, death, and resurrection. But when I try to do so, my mind gets blocked.

Luke's gospel talks of those times when Satan tries to block the good news through persecution and more. When I experience those times, I pray for God's guidance, and the Holy Spirit helps me through "witness block." The right words come from within.

—Cathy Mayfield

*Jesus, remove any block standing in the way
of sharing Your love with others.*

support

And God made the beasts of the earth according to their kinds. . . . And God saw that it was good. —Genesis 1:25 (RSV)

My married friends needed support. Their large yellow Labrador, Buddy, looked from husband to wife. His master, Ron, had a big bandage on his leg and could not walk the dog as he usually did. His mistress, Jo, was sitting at the dining room table bent over a large three-ring notebook with instructions about how to care for a patient who had just had a knee replacement.

Support: a strong word, a fortifying word, one that reminds us of all the ways God sends help when we need it. Buddy got up and padded over to his master and licked his hand. Ron smiled for the first time since his knee surgery and reached down to pat Buddy's furry head. Then the dog padded over to Jo, leaned against her gently, and rested his head on her arm. She put aside the hospital notebook and put her arms around Buddy's furry body. She hugged him for a long, long time.

—Peggy Eastman

Lord, when we are hurting and feeling helpless, You send us support through the pets that share our lives and ease our pain.

arrested

I looked and saw the glory of the LORD filling the temple of the LORD, and I fell facedown. —Ezekiel 44:4 (NIV)

Don't move. Be in awe of God in this moment. I see His majesty displayed in a breathtaking orange sunset over the blue-violet lake or in the delicate face of my young granddaughter. These gifts stop me in my tracks and remind me how much God loves us. Business as usual pauses for the divine.

The root "rest" can mean to stay still, but it also refers to being free from unease. God not only amazes with the beauty of His creation, but He also ensures justice. Wrongs will be righted. Selfish agendas dismantled. Even as Saul had his life redirected with a blinding light and a personal encounter with God, so can our hearts be purified as we are arrested in the presence of His radiant holiness.

—Tracy Smoak

Dear Lord, please lift my eyes to see You in all Your splendor. Amen.

coach

Show me your ways, LORD, teach me your paths.
—Psalm 25:4 (NIV)

Those who know me laugh when I remind them that I coached the high school golf team one year. Their laughter arises from the fact that I do not play golf and have only made one attempt at the game over my lifetime. What's even crazier is that my golf team won the league title that year—the only year that's been true for our school—and my son was named the league's most valuable player. My secret weapon was that I recognized that I knew almost nothing about golf, so I used teaching videos and sought help from others.

When we are confused about our life path and don't exactly know which way to turn for counsel, we can get the best coaching by going to God in prayer and the study of His Word. He never fails to provide instruction so that we don't head down the wrong path.

—Janet Holm McHenry

Lord God, provide a clear path for my future life steps so that my life truly honors You.

fear

There is no fear in love. But perfect love drives out fear.
—1 John 4:18 (NIV)

I slid into the seat of my car and trembled. My son's therapists had just told me my little boy needed to be tested for autism, and I was overcome with "what-ifs." What kind of life would he have? Would he be bullied for being different? Icy fear squeezed my heart.

"Mommy, sing to Jesus!"

I blinked away the tears blurring my eyes. Peering into the rearview mirror, I watched Nate's sunny smile and heard his sweet voice lift in song: "Jesus loves me. Jesus is mine . . ."

The one I was fretting over was lifting praises to God. I swiped away my tears and smiled. We sang song after song on the car ride home. With each melody, my fear evaporated. And I sensed God's love around me.

Fear cannot exist in the presence of Jesus. It scatters like darkness shattered by light.

—Tara Johnson

*Thank You, Lord, for loving us so purely. Teach my heart
to praise You no matter my circumstances.*

selah

You are a hiding place for me; you preserve me from trouble; you surround me with shouts of deliverance. *Selah* —Psalm 32:7 (ESV)

Selah. Bible scholars disagree on the Hebrew word's meaning. Some say the implied meaning is a musical rest or simply to "pause and reflect." Another interpretation is to "lift up, exalt, and magnify" the Lord.

Rest. Pause. Reflect. As a busy mother of eight, I never knew what it meant to relax. Widowed in 2012, I was thrust into a state of stillness I'd never experienced. For a brief period, before I needed a job to support the three children remaining at home, I allowed myself a time of solitude and silence. Grieving, I turned to God's Word, developing a personal relationship with Jesus.

Nine years later, children raised, I met Nick, a widower. Now married, we ask God daily to guide us, seeking to exalt and magnify the Lord in everything we do.

Selah. We pause each day in awe, thanking God for the gift of each other.

—Mary Potter Kenyon

Lord, be with me today. Let me pause and reflect before I speak or do, so that my words and actions might glorify You.

engrave

Behold, I have engraved you on the palms of my hands; your walls are continually before me. —Isaiah 49:16 (ESV)

After three pregnancies and two surgeries, I bear the marks of carrying and delivering life. Even if I wanted to forget my journey, I would be unable to, for the story of love and sacrifice is permanently etched on my body.

At times we may be tempted to feel forgotten by God, but He showed us His deep and lasting love in the nail-scarred hands of Jesus. Even on our toughest days, we can know that God has not forgotten us, for we are engraved on His hands. When we are tempted to doubt His care, we can pray that God will engrave this truth on our minds and hearts: that His love for us is as deep, lasting, and evident as scars.

—Heather Kaufman

Lord, burn this truth into my mind: I am engraved on Your very hands. Amen.

homecoming

For we know that if the earthly tent we live in is destroyed, we have a building from God, an eternal house in heaven, not built by human hands. —2 Corinthians 5:1 (NIV)

When my kids come home from college, it's a happy homecoming. I hang Welcome Home signs, cook their favorite foods, and enjoy watching them nap on the sofa. Their visits home infuse me with a jolt of motivation and enthusiasm. It's good to see their faces and have them rest at home. They feel safe and comfortable, and they know they belong.

I wonder if that's how God feels about us. I think of Him eagerly anticipating our arrival as he prepares an eternal home for us, standing at the door with open arms. Just as we arrange our homes for the arrival of loved ones, I imagine God preparing for our homecoming, when our earthly homes and our earthly bodies will be replaced by eternal ones.

—Prasanta Verma

Dear God, thank You for the exciting homecoming that awaits us at the end of this earthly life.

words

Do not let any unwholesome talk come out of your mouths, but only what is helpful for building others up according to their needs. —Ephesians 4:29 (NIV)

As a writer, I spend my day looking at words, scrutinizing their meaning, sounding them out, and rearranging them. I can string them into sentences where each one fits with the next like pearls on a necklace or compose pieces as clunky as a bracelet made from a child's pop-beads. The words I choose to write mold the way the world sees me. They also shape the way I see myself.

When I write words that are hurtful or could be misconstrued, it's easy to delete them. But the words I speak can't be called back. Once they're said, they carry the power to build someone up or tear them down. I pray my words reflect the wisdom found in Psalm 19:14 (NIV): "May these words of my mouth and this meditation of my heart be pleasing in your sight, LORD, my Rock and my Redeemer."

—Heidi Gaul

Lord, please guide my words, both written and spoken, to reflect Your love. Amen.

cling

Serve only the LORD your God and fear him alone. Obey his commands, listen to his voice, and cling to him.
—Deuteronomy 13:4 (NLT)

When baby birds hatch, they bond with the first individual they see. Usually, it's the mother. But when it's a person, the fledgling is misled to cleave to that individual—thinking of itself as a human. As a result, the bird will not mate, because it can't identify with its own species. It will reject them, clinging forever to its human parent—doomed to never reproduce.

I'm reminded of my own propensity to latch on to things that never satisfy. I replace God with idols in my life—activities, possessions, or relationships that bring me false comfort and peace. I embrace them, ignoring the love of my heavenly Father.

If I train my eyes and heart to look to the Lord, this is where my destiny truly lies. I was created to cling to Him alone.

—Tez Brooks

Father, forgive me for my tendency to serve idols.
Teach me to cleave to only You. Amen.

appointment

Then Moses said to the people, "Be ready for the meeting with God in three days." —Exodus 19:15 (ERV)

A s I cleaned out the desk in my law office, I found a stack of appointment calendars. Flipping through these books' pages brought back memories. Court hearings, board meetings, client appointments, business lunches, and medical appointments were noted. I'd carefully recorded their times because these events were important; I didn't want to miss them or be late.

While I'm disciplined about writing down and keeping appointments such as these, how diligent am I about scheduling and spending time with God daily? If I can set times to meet with clients and business associates, why don't I make more of an effort to schedule time with my Heavenly Father? I started to plan devotional and quiet time with God each morning. It's one appointment I enjoy keeping.

—Alice H. Murray

Dear God, an appointment with You is the most important appointment I can set any day. Amen.

smooth

The crooked roads shall become straight, the rough ways smooth. —Luke 3:5 (NIV)

After several harsh winters of snow and ice, paired with the salt treatment used to melt them, the parking lot outside the place I work was in great need of repair. After a notorious pothole threatened employees' cars, my boss hired a company to repave the lot, and the smell of fresh asphalt soon lingered in the air. When the job was finished, the parking lot was transformed—its rough patches gone and the surfaces now smooth.

God works in our lives in a similar way. We often have many metaphorical cracks and potholes that cause us to trip and stumble. Our sinful tendencies bring great heartache and pain. In addition, things like stressful work environments, relational problems, financial instability, and unexpected crises remind us of our frailty and desperate need of a Savior.

Praise God for the way He smooths our rough ways and makes our crooked paths straight.

—Mindy Baker

Lord, please make my rough ways smooth.

only

Blessed GOD, Israel's God, the one and only wonder-working God! —Psalm 72:18 (MSG)

I sometimes imagine my limitations hinder God. I'm only an obscure, sixty-something dreamer. How can God use me to make a difference? And then I recall biblical accounts of less-than-famous people God used to carry out His plans.

Noah had only his family to build an enormous floating farm. God gave them the strength they needed to finish the task. Moses's sister Miriam had only one instruction: "Watch over your baby brother." When she obeyed, miracles were set in motion that saved a nation. The unknown Israelite Jesus had only a dozen ragtag men to turn the world upside down. To this day, we feel the glorious aftershocks of their obedience to Jesus's words, "Go . . . and preach the gospel."

Since God is the same amazing God He's always been, He can work wonders through little me. And you.

—Jeanette Levellie

Dear Lord, everything I am and all I have, no matter how small, I offer to You. Amen.

haplotes

The testimony of our conscience that we conducted
ourselves in the world in simplicity and godly sincerity,
not with fleshly wisdom but by the grace of God.
—2 Corinthians 1:12 (NKJV)

My heart can become divided—desiring Jesus and more of His presence, but also striving for the things of this world. I find myself filling my wish list with store finds and my days with ways to get ahead. But God calls us to give Him our undivided attention, so when I'm drawn to the things of this world, my heart cries out for *haplotes*.

Haplotes is often translated as "simplicity," but a fuller definition of the Greek word gives us simplicity with the purpose of being devout: single-hearted focus on Christ. It was my word of the year a few years back. A call to seek God with my whole heart.

Haplotes has become a rallying cry for me. A prayer to live surrendered to Christ. An invitation to live in the fullness of God's plan for me.

—Crystal Storms

Jesus, help me to live out haplotes *and be
single-hearted toward You. Amen.*

extraordinary

Daniel . . . was found to have an extraordinary spirit.
—Daniel 5:12 (CSB)

M y grandmother lived a very simple life, yet she had an extraordinary heart for Jesus that made a huge impact on me.

Living on a fixed income, she used all her extra resources to cook, bake, and deliver countless tasty treats to family and friends far and wide.

Her kitchen was always fragrant. Her Christlike heart was always on display in the extraordinary way in which she used her gifts to bless those around her and glorify her Savior.

Nothing about her life was flashy, but the legacy she left for me was above and beyond the ordinary. I strive to be like her each day as I pray to use my gifts for God and have an extraordinary impact on those I meet. I want to be extraordinary in kind words, gracious actions, and a Jesus-filled heart.

—Kristen West

Lord, please fill me with an extraordinary spirit that always points people to You!

tears

*It was a fine cry—loud and long—but it had no bottom
and it had no top, just circles and circles of sorrow.*
—Toni Morrison

I have cried a lot in my lifetime. I've lost many loved ones, a few to untimely or tragic deaths. I've had many material losses, some of which were out of my control, while others were squarely my fault. For all the amazing joy I've experienced, I've cried buckets of tears and yes, experienced circles and circles of sorrows. Jesus, the "man of sorrows," knows all too well.

King Jesus was no lofty, earthly sovereign, insulated from the trials of humanity. He was hated, rejected, suffered sorrow, and was ultimately killed without cause. He experienced all the depths of human pain, demonstrated poignantly when he wept over the death of Lazarus and also in the garden of Gethsemane.

He cried bottomless tears of blood so that one day, I could be with Him in heaven, where there will be "no more death or mourning or crying or pain" (Revelation 21:4, NIV).

—Isabella Campolattaro

*Dear Jesus, as I sometimes shed tears of sorrow in this world,
please call to mind a tearless eternity in Your loving embrace.*

tangled

Be strong! Be fearless! Don't be afraid and don't be scared by your enemies, because the LORD your God is the one who marches with you. He won't let you down, and he won't abandon you. —Deuteronomy 31:6 (CEB)

Deadlines at work! Bills to pay! Family holidays plus church meetings and events to plan. Time is as short as my patience. My heart is dark as life overwhelms me. I see myself as a tangled mass of strings being pulled in so many directions. If one end is pulled, it tightens at another location, choking out another area of my life. Would it be better if I cut away some loose strings? How could I decide which ones?

Although these days can be overwhelming, I have to remind myself of God's presence as He walks with me, guiding and protecting. It is at these moments I must remember to breathe, to take in His peace and allow Him to control the knots and pull the strings. He will carefully snip away the loose threads and open up the darkness so that I can see the light.

—Darci Werner

Lord, when life is overwhelming and I am drowning in busyness and stress, remind me to breathe and take in Your Grace.

diamonds

. . . let your light shine before others . . .
—Matthew 5:16 (NIV)

Aunt Helen loved to watch birds come to the feeders outside her living room window. After Aunt Helen passed, my father began hanging a birdhouse in a tree near her graveside. He replaced the houses every couple of years. One year I bought a house, painted it a bright white, and we went out to hang it.

The day was dark and threatening rain. Using a shepherd's hook, we hoisted the birdhouse into the tree. As we left the cemetery, rain began to fall. I looked back at the white birdhouse shining against the dark trees.

I said, "It looks good up there."

He replied, "Like a diamond in a goat's ear."

I hadn't heard that expression before and laughed. I've remembered it ever since. Now that Dad has passed, when I recall things that he said and did, those reflections give back light like diamonds—or a white birdhouse.

—Nancy Schrock

Lord, I pray that my deeds become like
jewels to my family and friends. Amen.

store

I have stored up your word in my heart, that I might
not sin against you. —Psalm 119:11 (ESV)

M om, you're the best mom I've ever had," my seven-
year-old son said as I tucked him into bed. Never
mind I was the *only* mom he'd had. His words nestled
into my heart and prompted extra-tight hugs. Years later, when
teenage conversations weren't quite so tender, I recalled the
treasured words from my brown-eyed little boy.

The psalmist tells us to store God's words in our heart
to protect us from sin. Our heavenly Father knows we'll face
temptations and difficult days when we'll need His guidance
and protection. The Bible teaches us the ways He intends for
us to live and reminds us of His love, forgiveness, and salvation.
When we reflect on His treasured truths, we remember His love
and our resolve to obey Him.

—Jeannie Waters

*Heavenly Father, as I read the Bible, help me store
Your words in my heart. Amen.*

still

Be still, and know that I am God. —Psalm 46:10 (NIV)

For as long as I can remember, I've had a lengthy to-do list. Even now, as a semi-retired empty nester, I'm often too busy. I volunteer at a food pantry. Play pickleball. Preside over a book club. And housework never goes away. Laundry. Vacuuming. Grocery shopping.

Doing nothing? Such an idea seems almost impossible! Yet I know how important it is to be still. I make it part of my day now, first thing in the morning. I spread an exercise mat on the floor and open the drapes to let the sun shine in. Then I assume the stretching position known as "child's pose," knees and forehead on the floor, arms extended in front of me on the mat as far as they can reach. I breathe deeply, eyes closed. It's the perfect way to make myself be still and quiet. And the perfect way to listen for God's voice.

—Jennie Ivey

I seek You in the stillness, Lord.

miqveh

God called the dry ground "land," and the gathered waters he called "seas." And God saw that it was good.
—Genesis 1:10 (NIV)

Y ou have to be careful when the wind picks up," our new neighbor explained as he nodded toward the lake. I would see it in those first months at our new home: the temperament of the waters out our window. While one evening affords us a leisurely paddle in the canoe, the next brings whitecaps and crashing waves against the shore.

Miqveh was God's act of gathering the waters at creation. He pooled them up as ponds, oceans, seas, and lakes—including the one I watch daily. My heart can be as fickle as those waters—heaving on the winds of circumstance. But still, God gathers me up. He "miqvehs" every emotion and thought. He calms and quiets my soul. I can trust the One who commands these waters because, as Isaiah 40:12 (NIV) reminds us, He "has measured the waters in the hollow of his hand."

—Eryn Lynum

Dear God, when my emotions and thoughts rage in reaction, gather them by Your Spirit and compose them with Your truth. Amen.

pliable

Like clay in the hand of the potter, so are you in my hand. —Jeremiah 18:6 (NIV)

The pattern went like this: Make the day's plans. Face unexpected interruptions or inconveniences. Carry frustrations to bed. Wake up, repeat. With those frustrations came guilt about my occasional impatience toward people, as well as resentment about situations outside anyone's control. I reevaluated my approach to planning, and I began praying for a pliable heart.

Like clay in the Potter's hands, a pliable heart is responsive and moldable. It softens when stretched. It bends when pressed. Rather than stubbornly insisting on its own way, it willingly carries the impression of a gracious and gentle God. To be honest, I want that more than productivity or accomplished plans. So now, after preparing my plans for the day, I ask the Lord to prepare me for *His* plans by making my heart pliable toward His will.

—Michelle Stiffler

Lord, make my heart pliable, ready to make the most of any opportunity—planned or unplanned. Amen.

staff

Your rod and your staff, they comfort me. —Psalm 23:4 (NIV)

I enjoy hiking. I live in the Mojave Desert, amid surprising, varied, and often breathtaking scenery. However, the desert can be a dangerous and unforgiving place, so in addition to hiking necessities such as a water bottle, knife, whistle, and first-aid kit, I also take a solid, five-foot-long staff on my hikes. It steadies me when I climb or descend rocky terrain. I use it to brush aside branches and thorns. And if I ever encounter a scorpion or snake at close quarters, it may come helpfully between us.

I sometimes think of David's shepherd psalm when I'm hiking with my staff. I know what it is to be comforted by a handy, strong staff. So, I thank God for His protection, support, and defense, saying, "Your rod and your staff, they comfort me." They do.

—Bob Hostetler

Lord, let Your staff protect, support, defend,
and comfort me today. Amen.

knead

Whatever you do, work at it with all your heart, as working for the Lord, not for human masters. —Colossians 3:23 (NIV)

Around the evening "witching hour" I often find myself pulled too many directions. Kids need help with homework, dinner demands my attention. I realized one of those nights that what we're really craving is a purpose.

So now, we prep. The kids grab their safety knives and chop veggies and fruit, and I get started on dough. Any dough. Pizza dough for the freezer, cookie dough for treats, or homemade bread loaves are all fair game—anything that gets my hands working so that my mind can clear.

It's in those hours that our attention turns from picking on and poking at to accomplishing this and that. The tasks never last long, but they help us reset. Everyone feels they have contributed, and that their contribution is important. And as for me, I feel like I have kneaded out my tension, making room for God's calming peace, leaving me ready for the night ahead.

—Ashley Kappel

Lord, bless me with the manual labor
that lets my mind dwell on You.

flow

Whoever believes in me, as Scripture has said, rivers of living water will flow from within them. —John 7:38 (NIV)

The speaker for an event I had planned sent an email saying she could not come. Panic, then anger bubbled inside me. The event was two weeks away.

"Connect with the woman via a phone call," a friend advised. "But pray before you call. Get God's direction."

"Lord," I prayed, "I'm so angry about this, and I need your grace to flow through me when I talk to her."

The next day I felt enough peace to make the phone call. When the woman shared her reasons for backing out, God enabled me to sympathize, then encourage her. She agreed to pre-record her sessions. Our conversation ended with prayer.

Any plan can unravel; any relationship can fracture. That's why I need to pray daily, "Flow through me, Lord. Flow your grace through me. Flow your love through me. Flow your forgiveness through me. Flow."

—Denise Loock

Thank You for all the ways You love me, forgive me, and strengthen me, Lord. Let those attributes flow through me today. Amen.

feed

Look at the birds of the air, for they neither sow nor reap nor gather into barns; yet your heavenly Father feeds them. Are you not of more value than they? —Matthew 6:26 (NKJV)

I stood at the sliding glass door watching the birds—cardinals, blue jays, chickadees, and wrens—frolicking in our big cotton-wood tree. But I couldn't focus on nature's beauty that day; I was agonizing about our three children—where they were and what and how they were doing—especially my oldest daughter, who was in New York.

Suddenly I heard a distinct voice in my ear saying, "Keep your eyes on Me and feed the birds, and I'll keep My eyes on your children." I felt an immediate sense of peace, of consolation. I knew God would do exactly what He said He would do: keep His eyes on my loved ones. And on me. My job was just to feed the birds and to believe in His Word.

So we set up feeders and got birdseed, and from that moment forward, I've never missed a day of feeding the birds.

—Linda Elkins

Dear Lord, help me remember that You will always keep watch over me and my loved ones.

agency

But Moses said to God, "Who am I that I should go
to Pharaoh and free the Israelites from Egypt?"
—Exodus 3:11 (JPS)

I used to watch a TV show called *College Bowl*. Teams of
students from higher-level institutions competed to answer
questions in a variety of categories, with the winners receiving
scholarship grants.

One evening a young woman on a winning team was asked
what she wanted to do with her degree, and she answered
sharply, "My ambition is to marry a politician. It's the only way I
can have any agency in this world." I still remember that answer
and the tone of her voice. She was clearly repeating something
she'd been told all her life.

Like her, I want to try to have an influence in a damaged
world, and, also like her, I can't do it without agency. Agency is
the foundation of effectiveness, so of course I ask God for it in
every prayer. Instead of being listened to, I want to be *heard*.

—Rhoda Blecker

God of my ancestors, my family, and my friends, please give me
agency so that I can do Your work.

superlatives

For he who is least among you all will be great.
—Luke 9:48 (NKJV)

While working on ideas for a devotional on trees, I considered the theme of superlatives: the tallest tree, the tree with the largest leaves, the widest tree, the tree with the most foliage in spring. See a theme here? The bigger, the better.

How many will admit to wanting the biggest piece of pizza, the prettiest bouquet of flowers, the cupcake with the most icing? Our human hearts yearn for more and most. It's that thing the Word calls the "flesh."

As I turn my heart to God's Word, I also find superlatives, ones that bring me closer to walking in His ways. A teeny, tiny mustard seed—"the least of all the seeds" (Matthew 13:32, NKJV)—grows into a mighty tree. In 1 Samuel 16, David—the youngest of Jesse's eight sons—is anointed to become king of Israel. My least, offered to God, becomes the best I have.

—Cathy Mayfield

*Jesus, like Paul, who considered himself the worst of sinners,
I fall on Your grace, the best thing anyone can do.*

share

Is it not to share your bread with the hungry and bring the homeless poor into your house; when you see the naked, to cover him, and not to hide yourself from your own flesh?
—Isaiah 58:7 (ESV)

S haring smiles and both adorned in aprons, my dad and my daughter, Sophia, surprised us by preparing a wonderful breakfast. Using nearly every dish in our cupboards, the duo happily scurried around the kitchen. The charming table linens and fresh-cut flowers created beauty, while the homemade waffles, sausage, and cheesy eggs delighted our taste buds.

They served breakfast to nourish our bodies, but their expressions of joy and love filled our hearts. As Christians, we demonstrate God's love whether we provide food for people in need within our community or cook a meal for our family. We can share a hug, a meal, or an act of kindness to bless others. As we share and serve others, we are spreading the message of God's love.

—Dawn Bata

Father, give me a heart to serve others and to freely extend Your mercy and grace. Amen.

shape

And we all, with unveiled face, beholding the glory of the Lord, are being transformed into the same image from one degree of glory to another. For this comes from the Lord who is the Spirit. —2 Corinthians 3:18 (ESV)

If you were to look at my leg just above the ankle, you might think something is wrong. My ankle is skinny, but just above that my leg curves out like a balloon. It looks like my leg is swollen, hurt. But nothing is wrong. I'm a professional Rollerblader who has skated so much, for so long, that my leg has permanently shaped to the curve of my Rollerblade boot.

I truly hope that, in the same way my boot has shaped my leg, Christ is shaping my heart. I hope I have worn His love so much, for so long, that my heart looks transformed. I hope that my heart looks like Him in the way I show love, grace, and mercy.

—Liz Hetzel

Lord, press on my heart with Your love, so that it will be transformed into the shape of You. Amen.

everlasting

Yea, I have loved thee with an everlasting love: therefore with lovingkindness have I drawn thee. —Jeremiah 31:3 (KJV)

Years ago, we moved from the middle of town to two acres in the county. Our new yard had trees, critters, and flowers. One type of flower that adorned it was unique: Its leaves were waxy like a succulent, and the dainty flowers changed from year to year. Some years they were purple, others pink, and then white. My neighbors called the flower by different names: "live forever" or "everlasting." Each year it returned, providing everlasting, never-dying beauty.

Everlasting is a fabulous one-word prayer. Scripture says God's love is everlasting. Everlasting never dies. Everlasting is, was, and always will be. God is the Everlasting God. He is always there for us. So I lift up the one-word prayer, *everlasting*, as a reminder that my love for Him is everlasting. My need for Him is everlasting. My worship of Him will be everlasting. I am in thankful awe because His love for me is everlasting.

—Nyla Kay Wilkerson

Dear Everlasting God, let me never forget that
You have loved me with an everlasting love.

refresh

The law of the LORD is perfect, refreshing the soul.
The statutes of the LORD are trustworthy, making
wise the simple. —Psalm 19:7 (NIV)

A working mom of four, I was exhausted. My teaching day started early and continued into the evening as I corrected students' essays. Extra duties ate into after-school hours, so I thought I didn't have time for reading my Bible and praying. But as weight gain and lack of exercise began to take a toll on my body and mental state, I knew I needed to pursue a more disciplined lifestyle.

I decided to get up a bit earlier, read my Bible, and then go walking. As I walked, I prayed. Eventually I found that even with an hour less sleep, I felt more energetic and refreshed. God's Word would fill me up with encouragement. And as I interceded for my community, my own worries dissipated. More than twenty years later, I continue to find that God refreshes me every day as I seek him in His Word and prayer.

—Janet Holm McHenry

Lord, each day You refresh my body and soul as I pursue You through prayer and the study of Your Word.

dog

God is love. —1 John 4:8 (ESV)

M y dog acts in opposites. Although her breed is a retriever, she's more of a *receiver.*

Waiting to *receive* her breakfast. Lingering under the cooktop to *receive* stray crumbs. Flopping over to *receive* scratches to her tummy.

Furthermore, though she'll run to retrieve a ball, she returns to wait—toy held tightly, tail wagging—as if to say, "See? Now how about some praise!"

I've resorted to calling her my Golden Receiver. After all, not only does she desire what's due her, but she's faithfully *received*—held in confidence—secrets shared when curled beside me as I confess sin. She's *received*—always with patience—my frustrations when I failed to hold back. And always with grace and love.

You know, apparently my good dog is a lot like my good God. And that, too, simply makes sense.

—Maureen Miller

*God, help me love like You. Perhaps I should retrieve
my Bible and see what it says. Amen.*

footprints

Your way went through the sea and your path
through the vast water, but your footprints were unseen.
—Psalm 77:19 (CSB)

Waves of anxiety crash against my chest. This is the fourth time in two months my husband has been in the hospital. His fainting at our local YMCA opened the floodgates of one health crisis after another: blood clots, A-fib, and now kidney cancer.

Staring at my Bible, I question whether there might be some solace in these sacred pages. Praying, I focus on Psalm 77:19. *Footprints.* God's footprints. Right in front of me—I just can't see them. Supernatural peace calms my fears as I allow this truth to bathe my soul. God is going before me, clearing a path on this frightening journey. By faith, I place my hand in His as He leads me step by step.

—Kathy McInnis

Sovereign Lord, thank You for Your unseen footprints of grace.
Teach me to trust You step by step, hour by hour, as
You guide me through this uncertain time.

sharpen

As iron sharpens iron, so one person sharpens another.
—Proverbs 27:17 (NIV)

How could I say no? What an honor to be asked to film a monthly Bible study with two close writer friends. But on camera? I was just a writer.

Somewhat nervous, I plunged ahead with the project. Sitting at my friend's dining room table filming the modules, I felt at ease. The three of us knew each other well, and we enjoyed talking about Scripture. I almost forgot I was on camera.

During our discussions, interesting points were raised. While the three of us didn't always agree, we thoughtfully, and civilly, presented our positions. I was inspired to dig deeper to prepare for each month's study and to investigate discussion points post-filming.

I realized later that my friends were sharpening me, encouraging more intensive Bible study on my part. No wonder God wants His children to regularly engage in fellowship with other believers. We help each other grow!

—Alice H. Murray

Dear God, thank You for the fellow believers who sharpen us in our faith journey. Amen.

silk

*Therefore, as God's chosen people, holy and dearly
loved, clothe yourselves with compassion, kindness,
humility, gentleness and patience. —Colossians 3:12 (NIV)*

Legend has it that silk was discovered by Chinese Empress
Leizu around 3000 BC. In one account, she was drinking tea
when a cocoon fell into her cup and began to unravel. She
spun the threads, invented a loom, and produced the first silk
garments. Silk-making eventually led to a four-thousand-mile
trade route called the Silk Road. But although silk is beautiful, it
eventually fades and decomposes; it's a temporary covering.

Each morning we must decide what clothing to wear for the
day. Likewise, we are not magically bestowed with the virtues
of compassion, kindness, humility, gentleness, and patience;
we must intentionally choose to clothe ourselves with these
life-giving qualities. Like the highly prized silk that inspired
people to travel the globe, these virtues have a value that is
recognized all over the world—virtues that reflect the eternal
nature and character of God.

—Prasanta Verma

*Dear Lord, please help me to clothe myself with compassion,
kindness, humility, gentleness, and patience each day. Amen.*

penetrate

For the word of God is alive and active. Sharper than any double-edged sword, it penetrates even to dividing soul and spirit, joints and marrow; it judges the thoughts and attitudes of the heart. —Hebrews 4:12 (NIV)

I arose after a long, restless night. My husband and I had gone to bed angry. A small incident had escalated into a full-blown fight, and we climbed into bed silent and sullen.

The next morning I opened my Bible and began to pray. I invited God to search my heart and reveal any sin that might be lurking there. Then I prayed, "If I'm at fault in this disagreement, please show me." I was confident my husband was wrong and I was right, but it seemed spiritual to pray, just in case.

Almost immediately God brought to mind the unkind words I'd said the day before. And my selfish attitude, which had demanded that we do things my way. Within minutes God had penetrated my heart with His Word and brought me to humble repentance.

—Lori Hatcher

Lord, my heart often deceives me. Penetrate it with Your Word and enable me to live in joyful fellowship with You and those around me. Amen.

cast

Cast your bread upon the waters, for you will
find it after many days. —Ecclesiastes 11:1 (ESV)

C asting bread on the water" means to give generously without worrying about what happens to the things we're giving. That's hard when we are prone to ask, "Will it go to the right cause? Will I hear about a return on my investment?"

But God's economy is nothing like the world's. The Lord wants us to cast, expecting nothing in return—not even information or confirmation. No strings attached. When we give money, goods, or services to others, whether discounted or free, our goal is not to receive something in exchange.

Yet so often I'm curious. Looking, waiting for my charity to produce some kind of return, I suppose? At least a thank-you note? While it's true we can never outgive God, and He usually does bless us for being generous, rewards are never to be our motive. The greater joy is found in benevolence without looking back. That is true generosity.

—Tez Brooks

Father, help me surrender my desire for recognition and affirmation by casting my gifts without seeking a return. Amen.

veil

And we all, who with unveiled faces contemplate the Lord's glory, are being transformed into his image with ever-increasing glory. —2 Corinthians 3:18 (NIV)

Though it was many years ago, I vividly remember my wedding ceremony. My bride entering the chapel. Her walk down the aisle on her father's arm. And that moment when I heard the words, "You may kiss the bride," and my new wife lifted the veil from her face, and we gazed at each other before we kissed.

As her love and beauty transformed me then, I pray that my Savior's love—and my love for Him—will transform me now and in the future. By faith I approach Him, lifting the veil between this world and His eternal presence, "that I may dwell in the house of the LORD all the days of my life, to gaze on the beauty of the LORD and to seek him in his temple" (Psalm 27:4, NIV).

—Bob Hostetler

Lord, let me, with unveiled face, gaze on Your beauty and be transformed into Your likeness. Amen.

everything

Don't worry about anything, but in everything, through prayer and petition with thanksgiving, let your requests be made known to God. —Philippians 4:6 (HCSB)

My dog and I were walking when a young woman stopped and asked if I had seen a card she'd lost with all her private information.

I told her I hadn't seen it but offered to pray that we would. I told her God cares about everything that has to do with His children. I asked the Father to show us where it was and thanked Him ahead of time for revealing it.

As I resumed my journey, twenty feet in front of me a light-blue card caught my attention. When I picked it up and gave it to the woman, she looked at the card, then back at me, shook her head, and said, "Oh my. Oh my."

God may be running the cosmos, but nothing we care about is insignificant. He wants us to pray about everything.

—Les Burnette

Thank You, Father, for caring about everything that has the least bit impact on us. In Jesus's name, amen.

nothing

For with God nothing shall be impossible. —Luke 1:37 (KJV)

Nothing. *I have nothing to wear,* my teenage daughters' voices echo. Convincing them otherwise seems impossible. Even with a closet full of clothes, they see no possibilities.

Isn't that just like us adults? Our vision of the impossible versus possible is skewed by our lack of understanding of who God is. Like my teenagers' limited vision of their closet, so is our understanding of God's power. He is the God of the impossible. Believing in Him allows us to experience His indescribable joy, victory in life's difficult seasons, and His provision in our lives.

How can we experience His power in our daily lives? In my practice, I pray and ask God to open my eyes to His power and goodness, and He does. He has proven to me that nothing, absolutely nothing, is impossible with God.

—Dawn Bata

Dear Father, help my eyes to be open to see all the possibilities of what You can do in my life. Amen.

contend

I will contend with those who contend with you.
—Isaiah 49:25 (NIV)

love movies and novels that depict battles for justice in courtroom scenes. One of my favorites is *Just Mercy*, a book by Bryan Stevenson that was later turned into a movie. It tells the true story of how Stevenson, as a young defense lawyer, went to Alabama to contend for a man named Walter McMillian, who was sentenced to die for a murder he didn't commit. Racism was at the heart of why he was falsely accused, and he desperately needed an advocate to help prove his innocence.

It is a satisfying feeling to watch a powerful defense attorney use his wit and power to contend with a ruthless prosecutor in order to help the falsely accused underdog receive the justice he deserves.

Do you have a situation in which you have been falsely accused or are being treated unfairly? Invite God to contend with your adversary on your behalf.

—Mindy Baker

Lord, my enemies are too strong for me.
Contend with them on my behalf.

unfamiliar

I will lead the blind by ways they have not known, along
unfamiliar paths I will guide them. —Isaiah 42:16 (NIV)

One foggy winter night, I was driving home with my then-ten-year-old son, CJ. We could hardly see the road signs and streetlights. He asked, "Mom, are we lost?" I assured him, "I know the way. Trust me." The thick shroud of winter elements made landmarks unfamiliar. I drove cautiously to make certain I would find my designated turn. We arrived safely.

However, there have been other times in my life when circumstances overwhelmed me and I prayed, "God, I have not been down this path before. I feel lost." It's then that I need to stop and listen for His direction. I feel His peace when I acknowledge I can trust Him. He already knows the way.

—Loraine McElhaney

God, I know this path on earth is not always predictable.
Help me to trust You through the unfamiliar.

cease

He makes wars cease to the end of the earth; He breaks
the bow and cuts the spear in two; He burns the chariot
in the fire. —Psalm 46:9 (NKJV)

Headlines blare that nations rage and waters roar.
Newscasts relay another tragedy has occurred. Leaders
declare war is near. Yet the One who makes wars to
cease calls me to stop striving and worrying about bad news
from far away. To be still and know. Know that He is able. Know
that He is with me, within me, and the One who sustains me.

When fears distract, my heart cries out, *cease*. Be still and
know that God is in control. Realign my heart with the knowledge that He is bigger than my fear.

When worries turn my eyes away, I pray, *cease*. Turn my eyes
back to Jesus. With my gaze on Him, peace replaces my natural
response.

When my heart becomes restless, I call out, *cease*. Rest in
His embrace. Then I can move forward from a place of stillness.

—Crystal Storms

*Jesus, help me to cease doing things on my own. Give me
grace to cease striving and rest in Your embrace. Amen.*

enough

The jar of meal was not emptied, neither did
the jug of oil fail. —1 Kings 17:16 (NRSVUE)

O ver the years we have welcomed many children into our home through foster care. But when our case-worker asked us to host a young boy with special needs, I hesitated. His list of medical diagnoses was intimidating, and my hands already felt full with five other children. I was poised to say *no* when the Lord reminded me of the widow of Zarephath. Elijah asked for her last bit of water and oil, and because she gave what little she had, her supply never ran out. Through this story, I felt God prompt me to say *yes*.

We welcomed this boy into our family, and at times it was difficult. But like the flour and oil, our time and love did not run out. Like God did for the widow of Zarephath, He provided all we needed. When God calls us to something, He provides enough.

—Kate Rietema

*Help me trust, Lord, that Your provision is enough
for the task You've given me. Amen.*

bruised

No discipline seems pleasant at the time, but painful.
Later on, however, it produces a harvest of righteousness
and peace for those who have been trained by it.
—Hebrews 12:11 (NIV)

My daughter stood with her hands on her hips in full toddler fury. "Mean Mommy!" she exclaimed. We were standing in the parking lot where she'd nearly been hit by a car. Thankfully, I had grabbed her arm and yanked her back to safety. Still, my passionate little one was clearly angry. I had imposed on her freedom, bruised her arm, and ruined whatever escapade she'd been about to embark on.

I have bruises. Marks on my heart and wounds to my soul. In complete frustration I've stood with my arms on my hips in full human fury. "Mean God!" And yet He looks at me tenderly, knowing my little escapade had doom written all over it. While I was hurt, the small bruise prevented catastrophe. He saves. He protects. He does it over and over again. We can trust Him.

—Elsa Kok Colopy

*Lord, help me to know that even when I feel bruised, Your
protection has saved me. I am forever grateful. Amen.*

wells

Isaac reopened the wells that had been dug in the time of his father Abraham, which the Philistines had stopped up after Abraham died. —Genesis 26:18 (NIV)

I remember one day when I was a kid, Dad and Grandpa cleaned out the well in Grandpa's backyard. At one time the well would have been used for drinking water, but he wanted to use it to irrigate his garden. They went down into that dark, wet hole with a ladder and hauled out mud and debris. Cleaning out the well was a dirty job.

Many biblical stories happen around a well. One of my favorites is in John 4, where Jesus tells the woman at the well how to find living water. And in Genesis 26:18, Isaac digs out his father Abraham's wells because the Philistines have filled them with debris.

Sometimes I feel my personal spiritual wells filling with modern society's debris. When that happens, I have to work to clear out my wells so that I can more freely access the living water.

—Nancy Schrock

Lord, help me to keep my spiritual wells
flowing with Your living water. Amen.

snore

Snoring keeps the monsters away. —Judy Blume

When my decades-long marriage ended in divorce, my life changed in ways too numerous to count. Many of them were negative, but there was one change I knew I was going to enjoy: *No more snoring keeping me awake!* I could climb into bed alone, turn out the lights, and revel in the quiet.

That's not what happened. Night noises in my new house bothered me. The icemaker dropped cubes every couple of hours. The heat pump clicked off and on. Horns honked and tires squealed. Nights when it was quiet were even worse.

"Help me, Lord," I prayed.

"Why not rescue a dog?" God whispered in my ear. So I did. Every night, she curls up on the foot of my bed and is snoring even before my head hits the pillow. Listening to her breathe, I fall asleep almost instantly.

—Jennie Ivey

I'm grateful, God, for the comfort of my four-legged friend.

epiphany

Look carefully then how you walk, not as unwise but as wise, making the best use of the time. —Ephesians 5:15–16 (ESV)

M y hand hovers hesitantly above the chessboard. I second-guess myself—or perhaps it is a third or fourth guess—before moving my knight. My six-year-old son intently watches, planning his next move.

In a game as leisurely paced as chess, you wouldn't think an epiphany would surface, but I've had a profound realization: this chess game with my son will be the most important part of my day, a strategic opportunity to create a lasting memory with my son. What if I played him again tomorrow? How many meaningful moments over this chess board might mark his childhood?

God grants these epiphanies of how best to spend the time He has given us. I can use these realizations to make intentional choices that will set the stage for a life well spent. I can identify these "time well spent" moments and make space for more of them—and maybe for more epiphanies down the road.

—Eryn Lynum

Dear Lord, fill my days with epiphany moments and show me how to wisely use the time You've given me. Amen.

hand

Yet I am always with you; you hold me by my right hand.
—Psalm 73:23 (NIV)

M y youngest granddaughter received a baby doll for her second birthday. As we left the restaurant, she was carrying her baby in a birthday bag in one hand and holding her daddy's hand with the other. He let go of her hand to take the bag, and our toddler took off running across the parking lot toward their car.

It struck me that this is what I do with God. I stuff my burdens in a bag. Then I head off into danger by myself, ignoring God.

God promises that He is always with me, holding me by my right hand. He knows what is ahead, and He loves me.

—Barbara Clobes Winfield

*Father, help me to trust Your hand and the guidance
You give me in all I do today. Amen.*

rule

Whoever has no rule over his own spirit is like a city broken down, without walls. —Proverbs 25:28 (NKJV)

I sat with a friend in a public meeting on a contentious subject. Before the meeting started, I told my friend, "Stop me if I'm about to do or say something stupid." He nodded, and the meeting began.

Soon I felt my blood boil and leaned forward, prepared to stand and speak my mind. My friend said nothing but placed a firm hand on my shoulder. I sat back and took a deep breath. Moments later, I stood and waited for the chairperson to recognize me. Though my comments that evening went largely unheeded, I took solace in having presented my case in the right spirit.

That friend has since gone to his eternal reward, but I have another Friend I rely on to rule my spirit and check my worst impulses. So I often pray, "Rule me"—especially in tense or demanding situations. Sometimes I'll repeat it over and over. And God answers, like a friend placing a firm hand on my shoulder.

—Bob Hostetler

Lord, rule me, today and every day. Amen.

abcs

Jesus replied: "'Love the Lord your God with all your heart and with all your soul and with all your mind.' This is the first and greatest commandment. And the second is like it: 'Love your neighbor as yourself.'" —Matthew 22:37–39 (NIV)

I practiced the alphabet as a child until I knew it by heart. As I grew up, I learned the ABCs of friendship, then marriage and motherhood. Those qualities became part of me.

When I was a young adult, the ABCs of faith changed my life. When Jesus spoke the two most important commandments, He laid a foundation I can live by. The simplicity of faith—to love God and love others—is beautiful and enlightening.

Today, as I feed the neighbor's cat, wrap a gift, or send a card to a loved one, I will keep these most important ABCs in mind. I will *abide* in Him, *believe* in the impossible, and *cherish* others. My life is simple, and so is Jesus's calling for believers. As simple as the ABCs. As simple as love.

—Heidi Gaul

Jesus, today I will Abide, Believe, and Cherish as You commanded. May I honor You as I bless others with love. Amen.

mother

As a mother comforts her child, so will I comfort you.
—Isaiah 66:13 (NIV)

When I was little, I suffered from severe asthma. The doctor recommended that I take steam baths, explaining it would help soothe my wheezing. Of course, my family didn't have a sauna in our home, so my mom would run a hot shower. The bathroom would become full of steam, and I'd have to sit in there for over an hour and breathe in the warm air.

I've never been one to enjoy the heat, so I was not pleased with this treatment. The air was so stuffy, and I felt hot and trapped. But luckily for me, my mom would always stay with me, sitting me on her lap and comforting me with her loving presence.

God is an infinitely more nurturing mother who comes and sits with us when we think we're alone. He never ceases to share in our suffering, filling us with comfort and calm—there with us always, no matter where we are.

—Roma Maitlall

God, you are my nurturing Mother as much as you are my protective Father. Comfort me when I'm in distress, filling me with the calm and peace only a loving mother can give.

repetition

Turn it, and turn it, for everything is in it. —Ben Bag-Bag

There are some books I have to reread every so often, and movies I have to watch every time they're on. I used to think the practice of returning to things I had already done was kind of a waste of time. I did it anyway; I still do, but I don't think I'm wasting time any longer.

I figured that out at the Torah study group in my congregation, which meets every Sabbath morning, and has for years. Over the course of a year, we read the five books of Moses. And the next year, we do it again. At the group study some time ago, one of the participants said, "Why are we studying this verse again? It hasn't changed."

The rabbi said, "No, it doesn't change. But we do."

That's when I realized that repetition isn't inert. It isn't just comforting in its familiarity. Every time we look at a familiar text and see something new, it's a way of showing us how we have grown.

—Rhoda Blecker

Thank You for providing me signposts along my path, Source of Growth, and for making me aware that they're there.

reinvention

Being confident of this, that he who began a good work in you will carry it on to completion. —Philippians 1:6 (NIV)

When God delivered me from excruciating tumor pain and dependence on prescription opioids, I began a two-part reinvention. My new life called for a paring-down of baggage I'd carried far too long in my heart, mind, and spirit. And of objects that cluttered the historic log cabin I call home.

During that time, a friend mentioned a song performed by Michael Card. A line in the lyrics focused me, guiding my every effort: "It's hard to imagine the freedom we find from the things we leave behind."* I played matchmaker, connecting beloved friends with long-collected vintage treasures. As I relinquished old Santas, stitcheries, and lamps to new homes, too much became just enough. My joyous cabin of content was God's seal of completion.

—Roberta Messner

You delight in reinventing us, Lord. Thank You.

*"Things We Leave Behind," written by Scott Roley, Phil Madeira, and Michael Card, 1994.

cover

He will cover you with his feathers, and under his wings you will find refuge; his faithfulness will be your shield and rampart. —Psalm 91:4 (NIV)

Her terrified shrieks filled the vehicle as we entered the car wash. Strapped in her rear-facing car seat, my daughter could not understand that she was safe. Her focus was on the strange noises and unfamiliar sights from her limited perspective. I jumped from the front passenger seat and hovered over her, blocking her view, sheltering her with my presence. My daughter was as safe as she had always been, but under the cover of my arms she now felt it. She focused on me, and her distress eased away.

In times of fear and uncertainty, when we cannot understand what is happening from our limited vantage point, we can cry out to God and ask Him to cover us with His peace. Like a bird with her young or a parent with a child, God promises to be with us. Under the cover of His presence, we can experience rest.

—Heather Kaufman

Lord, cover my anxious mind with Your Word. Amen.

salt

It is a covenant of salt for ever before the L O R D unto thee and to thy seed with thee. —Numbers 18:19 (KJV)

In the most unusual wedding I've attended, a pastor handed both the bride and groom a small cloth bag of salt. He instructed them to take pinches from their bags and sprinkle them into a third bag he held. "Just as these grains of salt cannot be separated," he said, "so your hearts are bound together in the covenant of salt."

I knew salt could be used for flavoring, healing, and preserving, but I didn't know until that day it represented a binding agreement in Old Testament times. The covenant of salt sealed the relationship between God and His people. Now, whenever I sprinkle a bit of salt on my food, I remember not only God's faithfulness to me, but also my complete dependence on Him. We are bound together forever in the covenant of salt.

—Tracy Crump

Lord, thank You for uniting my heart with Yours in an eternal relationship.

touch

She said to herself, "If I only touch his cloak, I will be healed."
—Matthew 9:21 (NIV)

When I visited my elderly mom recently at her senior living apartment, we shared face-to-face conversation as I showed her family photos. She appreciates the frequent visits from loved ones and shares with them what she calls her "favorite sport": a lovely meal in the facility's dining room. Mom relishes entertaining friends and family, because she looks forward to her "dessert": long hugs. That day she held fast to me for a several minutes before I had to go.

"There," she said. "I'm better now."

Sometimes the best form of healing comes from human touch—a hand on a friend's shoulder during a moment of tears, a two-handed shake, an arm across someone's shoulder. Jesus healed the woman with the bleeding disorder when she touched the hem of his garment. And perhaps my kind touch of another could provide heart healing to someone in need.

—Janet Holm McHenry

Because Your loving touch has healed my soul,
God, use me to touch the life of another.

bucket

The mind of a person plans his way, but the
Lord directs his steps. —Proverbs 16:9 (NASB)

H ow many times have we heard of folks making a bucket list—a list of any things they hope to do or complete by a certain time in their lives?

It's not that God doesn't want us making plans. He does. I just think He wants us aiming higher than completing this 10K race, or exploring a beach in the Bahamas, or watching all of John Wayne's westerns.

I believe God values "kingdom" plans. I think He values plans we make that draw us nearer to Him. Sure, for someone rehabbing an injury or getting in shape, put a 10K run on your bucket list. But consider making a spiritual bucket list: reading through the Bible in a year, volunteering at a food bank one day a month, or joining a small group at church. And if you don't attend church regularly, perhaps put that first on your list.

—Mark W. Salley

Lord, I pray, please direct the path of my life, however it may wind—and show me more wildflowers along the way!

prepositions

As I was with Moses, so I will be with you; I will never leave you nor forsake you. —Joshua 1:5 (NIV)

Explaining prepositions to an English-speaking student is hard enough. How would I ever get a non-native speaker with limited English to understand? As an ESL teacher, I had to figure out a way.

Using a dictionary definition wouldn't help. Even I had difficulty understanding what the entry meant. Then it hit me. Why not *show* my students what a preposition is?

First, I told my class that a preposition described location. Then I held a stuffed giraffe to demonstrate prepositions such as "on," "in," "at," "with," and "above." The students giggled, but they comprehended the grammatical concept.

Later, we read an Irish prayer during our ESL devotion time. The prepositions in it struck me in a new way; they described where God is for me. He's always *with* me; He's *in* my heart, *at* my side, and *on* my mind. He's everywhere for me—and can be for you too!

—Alice H. Murray

Christ with me, Christ before me, Christ behind me, Christ in me, Christ beneath me, Christ above me . . . Amen.

infinite

If the stars should appear one night in a thousand years, how would men believe and adore! —Ralph Waldo Emerson

---

I'd traveled to Churchill, Canada, to see the northern lights. What I didn't expect was that between the sporadic performances of the magical dance of the aurora borealis, I'd find myself so in awe of the stars. Somehow, at home, I'd come to take them for granted. But here, six hundred miles north of Winnipeg, the sheer number of stars visible in the ink-black night sky seemed infinite. Every night, looking up made me feel so very small.

But the stars are not infinite. The Psalms tell us God has counted, and named, each one. Only God Himself is infinite. What that one word describes is something that cannot be contained, measured, or even fully comprehended by my finite brain. Praying that word, and meditating on it, helps me keep things in perspective. God's presence is infinite. God's power is infinite. And so is His love.

—Vicki Kuyper

Lord, help my finite mind worship, and find rest, in Your infinite goodness and grace. Amen.

identity

But you are a chosen people, a royal priesthood, a holy nation, God's special possession, that you may declare the praises of him who called you out of darkness into his wonderful light. —1 Peter 2:9 (NIV)

I live in an East Coast metropolis where people from around the world migrate to enhance their resumes. When introducing myself to strangers at church, their first question is often, "What do you do?" For those employed in prestigious jobs, the answer confers prominence. But when I worked as a nanny for a few years, I avoided the question, even though it was the best job I ever had. Sadly, I had pinned my social identity to an occupation I had devalued.

Praise the Lord that in Christ, I am granted an eternal identity that is apart from any earth-bound occupation, whether "high" or "low." The Apostle Peter describes me as chosen, royal, holy, and God's special possession. I pray for the wisdom to identify myself and others using those descriptors.

—Grace Assante

Lord, help me to value my identity in Jesus and esteem others accordingly.

higher

As the heavens are higher than the earth, so are my ways higher than your ways and my thoughts than your thoughts. —Isaiah 55:9 (NIV)

Each weekday morning my father listened to Sky Watch Steve give his "eye in the sky" traffic report. As Steve buzzed about in his helicopter, he warned drivers to avoid congested thoroughfares and clogged interstates. He pointed them to safe roads that would get them to their destination quickly. My father trusted Steve and planned his morning commute based on his recommendations. He knew Steve could see things from the air that he couldn't see from the ground.

I'm grateful that God's perspective is higher than mine. All-seeing and all-knowing, He wisely charts the course of my days. He offers insight through His Word to guide me and orchestrates the circumstances of my life for my good and His glory. Because my perspective is limited, I don't always understand His ways, but I know I can trust Him.

—Lori Hatcher

Heavenly Father, help me never forget that Your ways are higher and wiser than anything I can imagine. Grow my faith and trust.

first

But seek first his kingdom and his righteousness, and all these things will be given to you as well. —Matthew 6:33 (NIV)

Reactivity. That is and always has been my biggest flaw. For too many years, for too many times, I have reacted rather than responded, in both my speech and my actions. Reaction is immediate, unthinking, automatic. Response requires pause, thought, deliberate action.

So, my one-word prayer is *first*. I need reminding to turn to God *first*, before I say or do anything I could regret later. *First* prayer, then words and action. I want to put Him *first*, before my immediate impulses, desires, or emotions, as well as *first* in my life, before all and everyone else. When God's will and his way are my *first* priority, all else will fall into place.

Before I begin my day, I want to remember to *first* spend time with the Lord, seeking His guidance. And before I end my day, to *first* turn to Him in grateful prayer.

—Kim Taylor Henry

Lord, hear my prayer of "first," reminding me to turn to You first and put You first in all my thoughts, words, and actions every day.

vague

After the earthquake came a fire, but the Lord was not
in the fire. And after the fire came a gentle whisper.
—1 Kings 19:12 (NIV)

Does anyone else wish that God was a stop sign? A clear, bright, definitive, direction-giving source. *Do not proceed. Do not move forward. STOP.*

Many times I have prayed for God's clear direction. "Tell me what to do," I've begged. "Send me a sign if this is the wrong choice." I can assure you that has never worked for me.

As I've grown, both in age and in faith, I've learned that God is a lot less like a stop sign and much more like a yield sign. *Pause here. Consider your surroundings. Move forward with caution and confidence.* As much as I'd like to believe that God will speak to me like in the Old Testament, with burning bushes and stone tablets, the reality is that God is much more vague when directing our lives. He doesn't dictate from above; He waits for us to seek Him.

—Ashley Kappel

*God, help me remember that Your silence isn't apathy. Help me
keep my eyes on You so that I may chart a clear path.*

bear

Praise be to the LORD, to God our Savior, who daily bears our burdens. —Psalm 68:19 (NIV)

When I got my first apartment, I wanted to decorate. I naively hung a shelf on the wall, artistically arranging some of my favorite collectibles on top of it. Unfortunately, I learned the hard way how important it is to make sure to anchor the shelf into the studs in the wall. I did not know that the drywall alone would not bear the weight of the shelf. Not long later, the shelf came crashing down, the collectibles broken in pieces on the floor.

Often in life we face difficult trials. Alone we cannot bear the stress, worry, or weight of the problems that we are facing. The good news is that we don't have to. Scripture tells us that Jesus offers to bear our burdens when we cry out to him for help. Praise God for such a loving Savior.

—Mindy Baker

Lord, thank You for bearing my burdens every day. Amen.

with

The best of it all is God with us. —John Wesley

My wife's parents were second parents to me. When my father-in-law began to have issues with his memory, he went to a specialist to be tested. His wife accompanied him. After the first battery of tests revealed signs of memory loss, the specialist had his wife sit next to him for a second round. She said nothing during the test, but with her nearby, his focus and recall improved substantially. The specialist later explained that she was his "anchor"; he performed much better when she was with him.

The presence of Jesus similarly anchors me. He is "'Immanuel' (which means 'God with us')" (Matthew 1:23, NIV). As the hymn says, "'Tis heaven to me, Where'er I may be, If He is there!"* His "withness" empowers my "witness." His nearness makes me fearless. "With [His] help I can advance against a troop; with my God I can scale a wall" (Psalm 18:29, NIV).

—Bob Hostetler

Jesus, be with me. Stay with me. Go with me. Amen.

*C. Austin Miles, "If Jesus Goes With Me," public domain.

adoption

He predestined us for adoption to sonship through
Jesus Christ. —Ephesians 1:5 (NIV)

When my husband, Barry, and I applied for adoption of our dog, Molly, we were unaware she came with emotional baggage. Because she is deaf, she has attached herself to us like Velcro. If Barry sits in a chair, she rests part of her body on his foot so that she will know if he moves. If we leave her alone in the house, she climbs onto the table and counters.

We have taken her to training classes, given her antianxiety meds, and used a vibration collar to help stop unwanted behaviors. Now we hear from a neighbor that she barks incessantly if we leave her, even for a short time. We love that dog—even with her faults—and so we patiently and lovingly work to teach her the right way to behave.

That experience made me realize God has adopted us. He frequently gets our attention when we are on the wrong track, but He has given us the assurance of His forever love.

—Loraine McElhaney

*Thank you, God, for our adoption through
Jesus and Your everlasting love.*

innocent

If we confess our sins, he is faithful and just and will
forgive us our sins and purify us from all unrighteousness.
—1 John 1:9 (NIV)

The one outstanding hallmark of babies is innocence.
Their sparkling eyes, reflecting how recently they arrived
from God's pure presence. Their ready smiles. Their
trust. But when they start preschool or kindergarten, they come
home with all sorts of "facts" we'd rather they didn't know.

Just as I wanted to keep my young children innocent, I've
often wished the same for myself. Never to have known the
meaning of certain words. Not participated in some of the ugly
scenes of my past.

And then I remember that I have Jesus. He daily cleanses
me of every sin, even the ones I committed after I chose to follow Him. He does the same for each of His children. When we
ask for forgiveness, He gives us back the innocence of a newborn. What a Savior!

—Jeanette Levellie

*Dear Lord, thank You for erasing all my wrongs
and restoring my innocence. Amen.*

simple

So continuing daily with one accord in the temple, and breaking bread from house to house, they ate their food with gladness and simplicity of heart, praising God and having favor with all the people. —Acts 2:46–47 (NKJV)

I tend to make things harder than they should be—adding complexity to problems, creating cumbersome processes, and increasing stress levels.

My heart craves the simplicity that is in Christ. To overflow with the peace that comes from His presence. To follow His command to love God and to love others.

When I become overwhelmed by it all, my soul asks: "How can I make this simpler?" When time doesn't allow for every step to be completed, I ask Jesus to help me understand what is essential. When I know there must be a better way, my prayer for simplicity leads me to His way.

A simple focus leads to gladness of heart. A simple life reflects Christ. A simple way points others to the way of Jesus.

—Crystal Storms

Jesus, lead me in the ways that are simple. Give me a heart of simplicity that overflows Your love and peace to others. Amen.

certainty

It was you who set all the boundaries of the earth; you made both summer and winter. —Psalm 74:17 (NIV)

As summer turns to autumn, the days become cooler, the maple leaves turn fiery red, and the yellow school bus rumbles down our road. The change feels comforting. Summer, autumn, winter, spring. The rhythm is predictable, dependable, certain.

But imagine how unsettling it would feel to watch leaves fall to the ground if we didn't know what was coming next. What if we didn't know the plan for weather to warm, leaves to unfurl, and spring to come again? It's easy to trust the faithfulness of changing seasons because we've witnessed this rhythm for as many years as we've been alive. Yet, if we take time to reflect on our own lives, we would see God's faithfulness through the years has been just as certain as the seasons. And because we've witnessed God's faithfulness in the past, we can live in certainty of His faithfulness for the future.

—Kate Rietema

Lord, I am certain I can trust You through the changing seasons of my life. Amen.

bread

Open your mouth wide, and I will fill it
with good things. —Psalm 81:10 (NLT)

I was so frustrated. I had done it again. Instead of running to my God when I was going through a hard time, I'd gone to food for comfort. My aching belly and unsatisfied soul left me feeling even worse than before. Why couldn't I learn that there was no true help in those broken hiding places?

I opened the Bible, and my tear-filled eyes fell on an old, familiar Scripture. *I am the bread of life.* The words pierced; the truth seared. And yet I felt oddly comforted in the midst of the correction. He is the bread of life. Like the fragrance of warm bread, He wraps me up. Like the nourishment it provides, He sustains me with His care. Better than any counterfeit, our God truly can meet our need.

—Elsa Kok Colopy

Lord, help me to turn to You instead of any other hiding place. You alone will sustain me. Amen.

follow

My sheep listen to my voice; I know them, and
they follow me. —John 10:27 (NIV)

I grew up in North Carolina—far enough south that snow
isn't commonplace, and far enough north that it's not a total
shock when flurries fall. When I was a little girl, there was an
ice storm that closed schools and businesses for a whole week.
The first night, while it was still snowing, I went for a walk in the
woods with my daddy. His heavy boots crunched through the
snow, leaving deep prints in his wake. I followed, stepping from
print to print.

My daddy had made a way for me, one that many times
kept me from tumbling into the snow. All I had to do was follow. I'm so grateful that we have a Heavenly Father, our Abba,
who does the same for us. He goes before us; He makes a way.
All we have to do is follow.

—Haley V. Craft

*Abba, thank You for the way You guide me. Give me
the strength and courage to follow. Amen.*

knock

Ask, and it will be given to you; seek, and you will find; knock,
and it will be opened to you. —Matthew 7:7 (ESV)

Knock. *Knock. Knock.* I glance from the couch to witness two neighborhood boys peeking through our glass door. *Knock. Knock. Knock.* Every Sunday afternoon a familiar rhythm occurs at our front door: a very persistent asking and seeking to come in and play with our son.

Isn't that similar to what God does as He knocks, metaphorically, at the door of our hearts? He asks and seeks to come into our hearts, our dwelling place. Just as the neighborhood boys persistently knock on our door, God fervently knocks and seeks a relationship with you and me. Unlike the noisy boys I allow into our home, God enters our dwelling place quietly. He hears our requests and longs to give us the desires of our heart. When we seek Him, we will find peace, joy, and contentment as He knocks on our heart's door, asking to come in.

—Dawn Bata

*Dear Father, help me to answer Your calling as
You knock on the door of my heart. Amen.*

secret

Do not reveal another's secret. —Proverbs 25:9 (ESV)

C an I tell you a secret?"
It's a question I hear a lot, perhaps because I've earned the reputation of being someone who keeps confidences. I learned to be a secret-keeper at my mother's knee. "If you make a promise to someone, you must keep it just as God keeps His promises to us," she told me. "And one of the hardest promises you'll ever have to keep is not telling a secret someone shared with you."

No matter how tempting it is to share the "juicy" stuff I know, I won't do it. Whether the secret involves a marriage, children, a job, a trip, finances, legal problems, or anything else, I keep my heart and my ears open when someone tells me something in confidence. And I keep my lips zipped. It's the right way to be a friend.

—Jennie Ivey

Make me ever mindful, Lord, of earning the trust of others.

eclipse

The light shines in the darkness, and the darkness
has not overcome it. —John 1:5 (NIV)

My husband and I watch speechless out the window as the mountain summit swallows the full moon. I've witnessed countless sunsets in my life, but never a moonset. To the east, the sun has yet to brush the horizon. Moments ago, the massive, full moon hung low to the west. But then our peaks—still shrouded in darkness—pierced its perfect orb. They eclipsed its mirrored light.

Unlike a sunset, which bleeds true color onto the horizon well after the sun has slipped behind the mountains, a moon's false light disappears with no trace. False light is easily eclipsed and stripped of its power, while true light cannot be concealed. With each turn of the world on its axis, God is training my attention toward His true light. He exposes false pretensions and ideas and—as consistent as the rising sun—guides me to the everlasting light of life.

—Eryn Lynum

Dear Lord, Your light cannot be eclipsed. Nothing can obscure it. Guide me in Your everlasting light. Amen.

visit

I needed clothes and you clothed me, I was sick and you
looked after me, I was in prison and you came to visit me.
—Matthew 25:36 (NIV)

Through the years, whenever I read or heard this passage,
I could easily relate to helping clothe people or visiting
the sick. But never could I imagine going to visit someone in prison.

That day came five years ago, when a judge sent our son to
prison for leaving the scene of an accident. For the next four
years, we spent many weekends in the prison visitation room.
As I looked around that room, I did not see criminals or bad
people. I saw children—including my grandsons—hug their
dads so tightly, not wanting to let them go. I saw the smiles
when we came in and the tears when we said goodbye.

Our son is home now. This terrible experience has changed
him forever, bringing him closer to God—and changing my
understanding of what it means to visit people in need.

—Elisabeth Rachel

*Lord, I pray that the visits continue for all prisoners
so that they feel Your love through them. Amen.*

ruin

*Lord, to whom shall we go? You have the
words of eternal life. —John 6:68 (NIV)*

For several years now, my wife and I have lived in the Mojave Desert, where many homes have rocks and dirt for lawns and a yard ornament of an old, weathered wagon wheel. None of these homeowners own horse-drawn wagons. The wheels long ago became too warped or worn for such use. But my wife would like to have a wagon wheel. However ruined it may be for travel, she would treasure it for the decorative look it brings to our yard.

Something similar happened to me, many years ago. I was preparing for a lucrative career and a certain kind of life. But, after surrendering my life and my plans to God, I was surprised to discover that He'd ruined me for that career and that kind of life. It was my destiny to be valued for a completely different reason than the one I'd intended.

Since becoming His treasured possession, I occasionally pray that word—*ruin*—as a way of asking God to ruin me for anything and anyone but Him.

—Bob Hostetler

Lord, ruin me for anything and anyone but You. Amen.

cymbals

Praise Him with loud cymbals; Praise Him with clashing cymbals! —Psalm 150:5 (NKJV)

When I was in high school, I played crash cymbals in the marching band; later, I went on to play cymbals in the Blue Knights Drum and Bugle Corps. Cymbals may not have been the most difficult or exciting instrument to play, but they always made an impact—loud and clashing. And back then, the cymbals were downright heavy to carry. I had to build up my strength to clash them together and lift them high, fanning them out for all to see.

It wasn't only the sound that made the cymbals unique. When I fanned them out on the field, everyone in the stands could see them and how they reflected the light. So when I hear Bible verses about praising God with loud cymbals, that's what I'm thinking of—reflecting God's light into the world, not only with sound, but also with the brilliance of my heart lit by the Lord.

—Deb Kastner

God, let my praises sound like a mighty cymbal, and may I reflect Your light into the world.

rescue

I have made you and I will carry you; I will sustain you and I will rescue you. —Isaiah 46:4 (NIV)

My family and I love action movies, particularly the ones that involve a high-stakes rescue mission. There's just something so exhilarating about watching a hero risk it all to save someone or—in many cases—save the world.

In a lot of ways, the Bible is the ultimate rescue story. Beginning with God's ancient promise to redeem Adam and Eve of their sin, the story culminates in the death of God's Son, Jesus, who lovingly offers to die in humankind's place. He's the hero of the story—the One who gives it all up to rescue the people He loves and fulfill the awesome mission He was sent out to do: Save the world.

Whenever I feel scared and alone, I envision Jesus coming to my rescue, marching through the thick of my life and delivering me from my present situation. I encourage you to do the same whenever you are struggling.

—Roma Maitlall

Jesus, You are our mighty Savior and Deliverer.
I feel scared and alone. Rescue me!

streams

He is like a tree planted by streams of water.
—Psalm 1:3 (ESV)

While cleaning our basement, I found an old devotional entitled *Streams in the Desert* that belonged to my husband's grandma. I was spiritually dry, physically exhausted, and in need of refreshment from God. The image of a stream flowing through a parched land reflected my heart.

I read the book daily over the next several months. As an antiquary and former history teacher, its worn pages and old-fashioned vernacular spoke to me. The author wrote that she struggled with trusting God, as I did. Yet her faith was intact. I felt well-watered after reading it, like a stream that gently sustains the plants and animals it touches. God surprisingly met my deeply personal needs.

God has a life-giving stream to meet your needs too. Ask Him to fill you with a personal stream of living water only Jesus can provide.

—Brenda Yoder

Lord, fill my soul with abundant streams of Your care.

predictable

For Jesus doesn't change—yesterday, today, tomorrow,
he's always totally himself. —Hebrews 13:8 (MSG)

Most of the time, I like things in order. I get up, make my husband's lunch, and have my devotional time. It's predictable. Our dog, Kenai, likes things the same way. He has his routine: do his business outside, get an animal cookie; watch as I make Kevin's tea, get an ice cube; say goodbye to Kevin, get his KONG—a treat-filled toy. It's predictable.

The troubles arrive when that predictable routine gets mixed up or waylaid. When my husband is off work during the week, it throws Kenai's world off-kilter. He doesn't get the toy he anticipates every weekday. He lays on his bed, eyes boring into my back as I make breakfast. My love for him—the love he's come to think of as predictable—didn't come through.

Ah, how grateful I am that my predictable sin is covered by God's more predictable love.

—Cathy Mayfield

Jesus, may others see Your predictable love in me,
no matter what is going on in my world.

scars

But he said to them, "Unless I see the nail marks in his hands and put my fingers where the nails were, and put my hand into his side, I will not believe." —John 20:25 (NIV)

A s I wandered the aisles of an outdoor flea market, a gust of wind blew my bangs every which way. I noticed a lady staring at the deep scar that stretched vertically from my hairline to my nose, a remnant of an old surgery. "I'm a makeup consultant, ma'am," she said. "If you'd use my foundation, you could just about hide your scar."

I'd had my share of makeup collecting in that crevice; it only made the scar more noticeable. Bangs did a fine job as long as the wind didn't blow through. Bangs, and what thirty-eight years of caring for our nation's veterans had taught me. Their scars were badges of honor that told what they gave for my freedom. Scars that made their sacrifice real for me.

Scars tell the stories of where we'd been. Of healing and being whole again. They say that we'd never been out of God's care.

—Roberta Messner

Scars tell the stories of Your constant watchfulness, Lord.

walk

And He walks with me and He talks with me / And he tells
me I am his own. —C. Austin Miles, "In the Garden"

Sometimes when I "exercise" walk, I tuck my cell phone into
my pocket and listen to upbeat music through my earbuds.
Sometimes I listen to podcasts or talk radio. And sometimes I listen to audiobooks. These distractions help me walk
farther and faster, which is usually exactly what I set out to do.

But I set aside time to walk with God, too. Quiet walks,
when I can amble along and take in the sights and sounds and
smells around me, whatever the season, whatever the time of
day. No counting steps, no hurrying, no electronic distractions.
Just God and me, walking and talking together in the beauty of
His creation.

—Jennie Ivey

*Thank You, Heavenly Father, for the times when You wrap
Your arms around me and tell me I am Your own.*

popcorn

What is the price of five sparrows—two copper coins? Yet
God does not forget a single one of them. And the very
hairs on your head are all numbered. So don't be afraid; you
are more valuable to God than a whole flock of sparrows.
—Luke 12:6–7 (NLT)

I am a movie lover. I especially like animated features.
Watching the big screen in a dark theater with a tub of hot,
buttered popcorn, I feel like a kid again. Munching on the
salty treat completes the movie experience for me. It's a little
thing, but popcorn brings such a contented smile to my face.

God created our world with many amazing, important
things. Today I am thanking Him for a small detail, the joy of
crunching popcorn at a movie. He cares enough about me to
give me the little delight of popcorn as well as the enormous
gift of the breath of life. I am a beloved daughter with salty,
buttery fingers.

—Lisa Bogart

Thanks, Dad, for popcorn! For loving us so much
You created little joys in every day. Amen.

shepherd

You were lost sheep with no idea who you were or where you were going. Now you're named and kept for good by the Shepherd of your souls. —1 Peter 2:25 (MSG)

Sheep aren't particularly smart, and they don't have natural defenses. I prefer not to be compared to sheep, but God didn't let me get away from that reality when I led a Bible study on Psalm 23. I had to admit, along with the rest of the study group, that I often feel like a lost sheep—alone, terrified, in pain, unable to defend myself.

Through the wisdom of many beautiful women of God, I was reminded that feelings aren't facts; God's Word is. The fact is that we are found, named, carried, cared for, protected, guided, and loved. We have a Shepherd, One who calls us by name and calls us His own. We have everything we need.

—Amy Wallace

Good Shepherd, hold me close and remind me that in You I have all I need. Amen.

pain

He will wipe every tear from their eyes. There will be no more death or mourning or crying or pain, for the old order of things has passed away. —Revelation 21:4 (NIV)

Like many people, I live with chronic pain. Some days are better than others, but on all days, pain is a reality of my life. I have found that acknowledging my pain, leaning into my pain, and bringing my pain before the Lord is more fruitful then trying to flee from or ignore it.

Physical, emotional, and spiritual pain are a reality for many of us. Today you could be in pain, or perhaps you are feeling the pain of someone you love. The good word of the Lord is that one day, all pain will cease. As the old world passes away, God will free us from all pain and suffering. Being honest and bringing our pain before God in prayer is the first step toward God's promised healing.

—Heather Jepsen

Lord, I bring my pain before You today and pray for Your healing touch. Amen.

place

But when you pray, go into your room, close the door
and pray to your Father, who is unseen.
—Matthew 6:6 (NIV)

A good friend told me the importance of having a place to pray.

My first chair still holds fond memories. It was a $5 special from Goodwill. It was in this chair I made my place to pray before my family got moving each day.

It was in that chair I began reading through the Bible, which I would do over and over again as the years passed. It was in that chair I asked God why my eleven-year-old son was diagnosed with cancer. It was in that chair I wrestled with financial debt and worry.

That was the spot where God met me every day. He never missed a day. Having a place to meet with God has been invaluable.

The practice of being in a solitary place for ten, twenty, thirty minutes each day reminds me where my help comes from . . . the Maker of heaven and earth.

—Mark W. Salley

Thank You, Lord, for always being with me.

leaky

But we have this treasure in jars of clay, to show that the surpassing power belongs to God and not to us.
—2 Corinthians 4:7 (ESV)

It was a beautiful day outside and I was excited for the chance to host a family luncheon on our deck.

In the midst of entertaining, I noticed one of the drink containers I put out was leaking, and a stream of lemonade was snaking its way across my deck. I internally chuckled, thinking of the parallel between this vessel and myself.

We are living containers filled with God's Spirit and His glory, but as humans, we also tend to be leaky—forgetful, easily distracted, and prone to drift. Daily hardships, temptations, and distractions can cause the leak to go from marginal to massive in a matter of minutes.

Positioning ourselves through prayer, worship, and daily Bible reading helps us to be refilled. Doing this ensures God will take care of all our leaks!

—Kristen West

I acknowledge I am leaky, Lord. Fill me up again today with Your Word, Your Spirit, and Your glory!

hidden

He reveals deep and hidden things. —Daniel 2:22 (NIV)

S itting in the dentist's chair, I fully expected to hear the usual, "Looks great! We'll see you in six months." Not this time. A tiny cavity had formed along my gumline, above an old crown. Without the dentist calling my attention to what I wasn't able to see, that tiny bit of decay would have continued to grow, causing pain and problems down the road.

Sometimes I'm blind to what I need to attend to in my own life. Praying the word *hidden* invites God to reveal to me any bad habits or areas of weakness that remain hidden from view. Either I can't see them . . . or I choose not to. Through the whisper of God's Spirit, the honest admonition of loving friends, or life-changing verses of Scripture, God faithfully brings my blind spots into the light.

—Vicki Kuyper

Lord, reveal what's hidden within me. Then, give me the courage to change for the better. Amen.

trust

Trust in the Lord with all your heart and lean not on your own understanding… —Proverbs 3:5–6 (NIV)

The doctor sat, giving my husband the test results and diagnosis. A tumor encased his carotid artery at the brain. Her voice serious, she told us the situation was concerning, but not yet dire. My brain shut off. All I could think was that this was definitely not what we'd planned.

At home we wondered aloud what we could do. The answer was nothing. Nothing but pray and trust in God for a good outcome. Trust had never been one of my strongest personality traits. But when there's no choice, well, I try.

My husband underwent more tests and doctor's visits. As time passed, we learned to appreciate the sacred value of our prayer life. Deep trust freed us like a parachute in this, another of life's free falls. We continue in faith, knowing God has a beautiful future planned for us. One built on the flexible, unbreakable foundation of trust.

—Heidi Gaul

God, thank You for the parachute of trust You provide during each of life's freefalls. Amen.

draw

No one can come to me unless the Father
who sent me draws them. —John 6:44 (NIV)

When I came to faith in Christ at age eighteen, my
first thoughts were for my family members. I wanted
them to experience the peace, joy, and purpose I
had found. I shared my favorite Bible verses. I left gospel tracts
in strategic places. I waxed eloquently on the finer points of
apologetics and theology. But I discovered not everyone was as
interested in following God as I was.

On a particularly discouraging day, I read Jesus's words in
John 6 and realized that while God calls us to share our faith,
ultimately, He would be the one to draw my family members to
Himself. That's when I began to pray, "Lord, draw them close.
Draw them away from all that will harm them and toward all
that is holy and good. Draw their hearts to you, your house,
and your people."

—Lori Hatcher

*Father, draw my loved ones and friends into a rich and deep
personal relationship with You. In Jesus's name I ask. Amen.*

Immanuel

The virgin will conceive and give birth to a son, and they
will call him Immanuel (which means "God with us").
—Matthew 1:23 (NIV)

I volunteer as a mentor to prisoners, correcting their Bible study lessons and writing them letters of encouragement. Some of their prayer requests and comments are heartbreaking. They write about the loneliness and pain of being separated from their loved ones. One prisoner named Mark wrote about unanswered letters and being kept in the dark as to the status of his children; about his ex-wives adding another bucket of silence into what has become a vast ocean filled with his tears.

What do you say to someone like Mark? What comfort can I give Mark, or anyone else? Along with my prayer for Mark and others, I remind them (and myself) that Jesus is "Immanuel, God with us." He's with Mark in his prison cell during his darkest moments, and He is with us as we navigate life with its ups and downs, successes and failures, sorrow and pain.

—Dale R. Yancy

Lord, I take comfort in the fact that You are with me, no matter what I face tomorrow or in the days ahead. Amen.

(em)body

I am the bread of life; whoever comes to me shall not hunger, and whoever believes in me shall never thirst. —John 6:35 (ESV)

Today, with the thirty-three-week baby in my womb and it being the one-year anniversary of the murder of six Asian women in Atlanta, I have been reflecting on bodies. I remember Michelle Go, pushed to her death into an incoming subway, and Christina Yuna Lee, stabbed in her New York City apartment. I feel the burdens I embody due to my appearance, along with the longtime stereotypes associated with being an Asian-American woman.

John 6:35 (ESV) says, "I am the bread of life; whoever comes to me shall not hunger, and whoever believes in me shall never thirst." Despite the mistreatment, abuse, and violence committed against Him, God meant for His Son's body to be for the nourishment and healing of the world. God likewise created my body, like His, for good. I am reminded that within my body, even amid the pregnancy pains, I am nurturing, embodying, and bringing forth new life.

—Kristal Hang Calkins

Lord, how might You want us to use our bodies to bring nourishment and life to our family, friends, neighbors, and spheres of influence? Teach us how our bodies are made to be good. Amen.

prize

I press on toward the goal to win the prize for which
God has called me heavenward in Christ Jesus.
—Philippians 3:14 (NIV)

I closed my eyes, held my breath, and pushed Send to submit my work to a contest. I don't know why I do this, setting myself up for failure. Even though I've placed in some contests, I haven't come close to winning in others. Failure stings and plummets my self-confidence, yet there's a slim thread of hope I'll win an award.

I recently read an article about famous "losers" for the Academy Awards, and I was surprised to see how many well-known actors and movies never won one of the awards. Many weren't even nominated. Nevertheless, the value of their work wasn't diminished in my eyes. Although it's nice to get accolades from other people, I realize my reward comes from God, and that's the most important prize.

—Marilyn Turk

Lord, help me to be worthy to win the prize
You've planned for me.

fragrance

Thanks be to God who leads us, wherever we are, on his own triumphant way and makes our knowledge of him spread throughout the world like a lovely perfume! We Christians have the unmistakeable "scent" of Christ.
—2 Corinthians 2:14–15 (PHILLIPS)

I work as the administrative assistant at a church where a weekly women's Bible study meets. After the ladies leave the building, I make sure the lights are off and the front door is locked. Yesterday, as I walked through the meeting room I breathed in the sweet fragrance of someone's perfume. "Ahhh . . ." I said, and thanked whoever lifted my spirits by their scent.

Then I wondered what type of fragrance I leave behind. Not of perfume or cologne, but of attitudes. When I interact with someone in the market, the bank, or online, do they thank me for the sweet reminder of Jesus I give them? Or do they hold their nose?

—Jeanette Levellie

Dear Jesus, please remind me to share the sweet fragrance of You every day. Amen.

flourish

The righteous will flourish like a palm tree, they will grow like a cedar of Lebanon; planted in the house of the LORD, they will flourish in the courts of our God. —Psalm 92:12–13 (NIV)

The community garden out my patio window is nothing to write home about when spring begins. But in a matter of weeks, I see hearty perennials start to bloom in a rainbow of brilliant colors. After they peek through the crusty soil and slowly reach the sun's gaze, each bulb flourishes thanks to sun, fertilizer, water, and pruning.

The same can be said for me. During some seasons, I feel discouraged, my dreams lie dormant, and I don't see much progress. But in others, my faith blossoms, my relationships thrive, joy bursts forth, and I'm at my peak. The good news is that reaching my God-given potential doesn't depend on what people see. On the surface, it often seems nothing miraculous is happening. But when I cultivate my relationship with God by abiding in Him, I will be in full bloom before I know it!

—Sarah Cole

Dear Lord, thank You for all the ways You help me grow in my faith. In Jesus's name, amen.

sail

A ship in harbor is safe—but that is not
what ships are built for. —John A. Shedd

When I was in middle school, my parents bought me a small sailboat so I could explore the sparkling waters of Lake Michigan. Sailing produced a certain thrill, but it also came with risk. Sometimes the boom smashed into my head while tacking, or I'd have to pump the tiller when I lost wind, or I over-trimmed the mainsail and capsized. I became tempted, at times, to keep the boat on the beach where it was safe. But that's not what the boat was meant for—it was meant to sail.

Sometimes I feel a stirring of purpose—like wind tugging at the sails of my heart to leave what is safe and take a new risk. Do you feel this too? God didn't give us life to sit on the shore and watch. When you sense a bigger purpose inside you, take a risk and set sail.

—Kate Rietema

Lord, help me live boldly, pursue my purpose,
and experience all You have for me. Amen.

design

For you created my inmost being; you knit me together in my mother's womb. —Psalm 139:13 (NIV)

We were all so proud of our creations. Several of my girlfriends and I had spent the evening watching an art instructor and painting a grove of aspen trees. While my trees were slightly bent where they should be straight, and my strokes looked more toddler than Van Gogh, I was proud. I stood back with a big smile. *Mine.*

We are God's creation. Thoughtfully fashioned, lovingly designed. And while our artistry is fully human, His is divine. No mishaps. No mistakes. Only loving, tender, thoughtful design. Woven in our mother's womb—eyes, smile, talents, quirky personality. Every trait lovingly bestowed. He needed no instructor; He knew exactly what he was doing. And when He was done, He stood back with a smile on His face, a twinkle in His eyes. *His.*

—Elsa Kok Colopy

Lord, thank You for how You've created me. Help me to be grateful for Your design. Amen.

YHWH

Hear, O Israel: The LORD our God, the LORD is one. Love the LORD your God with all your heart and with all your soul and with all your strength. —Deuteronomy 6:4–5 (NIV)

Deuteronomy 6:4–5 is known by the Jewish people as the Shema, a sacred prayer recited daily. What our Bible spells LORD—all caps or small caps—is actually the ancient Hebrew name of God, YHWH. YHWH has a complex and mysterious history that fascinates me.

I only learned recently that pronounced correctly, God's original Hebrew name YHWH sounds like a breath (check YouTube). The very thought of this fills me with wonder, recalling that YHWH breathed life into mankind (Genesis 2:7).

Jews hold this name so reverently that they avoid uttering it aloud, even spelling it G-d rather than presuming to express it. Over time the name has evolved into variations including Yahweh, Jehovah, and Adonai. As I reflect on this holy history, I am humbled to recall that because of Jesus, I can call this holy, holy God *Abba* or *Daddy*, as a beloved child.

—Isabella Campolattaro

YHWH, may we be reminded of Your unspeakable holiness.

move

When he had finished speaking, he said to Simon, "Put out into deep water, and let down the nets for a catch."
—Luke 5:4 (NIV)

My family has always enjoyed the occasional camping trip. During one trip we encountered a severe pop-up thunderstorm. We could see it coming; we had maybe fifteen minutes to break camp and take shelter. My dad began shouting orders to Mama and the four of us kids. We were spread out around our campsite—some in the tent, some packing up food by the grill, some down by the water bringing in the canoes.

None of us had the opportunity to hear the orders the others received. Neither did we have the time to try figuring out how the orders would fit together to achieve the goal. We just had to move, responding to my father's call. I try to take the same attitude about God's orders. I don't need to understand all the intricacies of God's plan, but when I receive an order, I need to move.

—Haley V. Craft

Lord, help me always be ready to move
without hesitation when You call. Amen.

peculiar

But ye are a chosen generation, a royal priesthood, an holy nation, a peculiar people . . . —1 Peter 2:9 (KJV)

Jesus never promised that his followers would fit in. He said the people who embraced his teachings would experience rejection, even martyrdom. And that we should count it as joy to share in the same sufferings He endured.

Today many Christians live in a way that's contrary to popular culture, living out a worldview that is different from that of non-Christians. Often we make lifestyle choices that are distinct from others, which sets us apart as "peculiar," but those choices are born of deep conviction and a love of God.

The Lord instructs us to shine as lights in the darkness: to live peculiar lives because we are not of this planet. The word *Christian* means "little Jesus" or imitators of Christ. Today, may we stand tall and live our lives so that we stick out from all the rest, pointing to the Savior.

—Tez Brooks

Father, help me to live a life set apart from
this world, so I may shine in the darkness. Amen.

pause

Pause a moment, Job, and listen; consider the wonderful things God does. —Job 37:14 (GNT)

When I was a child, there was no such thing as a remote control to operate the TV. Instead, we turned knobs that were actually on the cabinet. Now, things are radically different. My TV remote has many buttons, and I don't have a clue what most of them do. But I recognize the Pause button. It's the one with two parallel vertical lines. When I touch that button, everything on the screen goes still and quiet.

I often use the Pause button to freeze the TV screen. But I use it in other parts of my life too. When I'm hurried and harried, with too much to do and not enough time to do it, I picture those two parallel vertical lines in my mind. *Pause*, I whisper to myself. And then I listen for the voice of God.

—Jennie Ivey

Remind me, Lord, to pause and listen.

bushwhack

My steps have held to your paths; my feet have not stumbled. —Psalm 17:5 (NIV)

Loose pebbles and dry pine needles slip under my boots; it is a natural rug pulled by gravity from beneath my feet. I catch myself before I fall, returning my attention to my daughter, who scrambles up the steep hillside in front of me. My husband is farther ahead with our three sons. We practice bushwhacking—hiking without a trail through the wilderness— often as a family. But this hike, with a lofty 350-foot ascent, river crossing, ice maneuvering, and dusk setting in around us, meets us with a new set of challenges. Together we carefully maneuver through the forest, practicing wilderness safety and navigation.

At last the trees open at the top of the hill to a sweeping view. Mountains stretch out all around us. The half-moon greets us from directly overhead. Navigating uneven ground is never easy—not on a mountainside or in life's circumstances. Yet God leads me over every obstacle. His strength is enough for each challenge. He steadies my steps as I follow His lead.

—Eryn Lynum

Dear Lord, help me to trust You on uneven ground. Amen.

caregiving

Assuredly, I say to you, inasmuch as you did it to one
of the least of these My brethren, you did it to Me.
—Matthew 25:40 (NKJV)

I n the early 1990s, my dear father had a crippling stroke. With the support of my family, he came to live in our home for twelve years. I wouldn't be truthful if I were to say each day was a cinch and delightfully fulfilling.

Caregiving can be fraught with trials and tribulations. However, there is a flip side. There were the daily smiles that greeted me in the morning, the gratitude on my father's face when I helped him get dressed, the quiet comfort of sitting together watching a San Francisco Giants baseball game and eating his favorite bean burrito with extra sour cream at lunchtime.

God promises to give us what we need to meet life's challenges. And, in those sweet, simple moments sprinkled throughout the day, you realize that what you are doing in a caregiving capacity is showing the love of God in a profound way. For this, I am deeply grateful.

—Ellen Akemi Crosby

*Thank You, Lord, for helping me be a reflection of
Your love to the world.*

risk

If you are not willing to risk the unusual, you will have to settle for the ordinary. —Jim Rohn

Redheaded Avery was four years old, the youngest in the family, as we entered a trailhead at Red Rock Conservation Area in Nevada. Her two older siblings and two older cousins started to clamber up the imposing rocks ahead, but Avery halted. Her eyes widened. "I'm scared." Her voice trembled. Seconds later, she propped her fists on her hips. "But I'm doing this!" Then she bounded after the others, conquering not only the rocks but also her fears.

I pray to be more like Avery, sometimes with the single word, *risk*, remembering how *The Voice* version paraphrases Jesus's words in Luke 9:24: "If you try to avoid danger and risk, then you'll lose everything. If you let go of your life and risk all for My sake, then your life will be rescued, healed, made whole and full."

—Bob Hostetler

Jesus, let me risk all, willingly and boldly,
for Your sake today. Amen.

illuminate

For You are my lamp, LORD; and the LORD illuminates
my darkness. —2 Samuel 22:29 (NASB)

As a child, whenever a storm created a power outage, Mother's remedy was to light the antique oil lamps and place them on top of the old upright player piano. It was the perfect placement for shedding light throughout our farmhouse. I felt as though the golden glow of the lamp pushed back the lightning of the storms, bringing me comfort. My sister and I would play the piano, accompanied by nature's tune of raging wind, pouring rain, and rumbles of thunder. When the storm's intensity grew violent, Mother's comforting words and the oil lamps lit our path down the stairs to the safety of the cellar. Even then, in the cold, damp space, the glow of the lamps warmed the night.

Today I know that as long as I have the glow of God's Word to light my path, regardless of how difficult a circumstance is, the storm always passes.

—Mary Hansen

*Lord, when the storms of life rage, guide me to safety
with the radiant light of Your words. Amen.*

clean

Create in me a clean heart, O God, and renew
a steadfast spirit within me. —Psalm 51:10 (NKJV)

We have lived in our current house for over twenty years now, and in that time have amassed quite a bit of junk, so recently I've been working on decluttering and then deep cleaning those areas I've decluttered.

It isn't as easy as I thought it would be. Even things I haven't looked at in years are hard to let go of—precious memories of times gone by when my own children were young. Now I have grandchildren who add to those precious memories. But I'm learning through this process that I have to let stuff go in order to truly clean.

I think my heart is much the same way. I have a lot of junk piled up in my heart, mind, and spirit that I just need to let go of, and only God can help me in this. He is the One who washes my sins away. When I'm feeling weighed down, He cleans all that gunk away.

—Deb Kastner

Scrub my heart clean, O Lord. Give me
a new spirit to better serve You.

pour

For I will pour water on him who is thirsty, and floods on the dry ground; I will pour My spirit on your descendants, and My blessing on your offspring. —Isaiah 44:3 (NKJV)

H ave you ever tried to pour a drink for a thirsty child who is holding their own cup? In their eagerness for relief, they almost always move the cup here and there, in a failed attempt to help you pour faster. Every time, you have to remind them, "Be still!"

I believe that there is a desperately thirsty child deep down inside me. I gasp and cry out to G-d for relief, but I am too parched to hold still. Rather than waiting for Him to grant me respite, I stand, dehydrated in an ocean of spilled blessings and unopened gifts, raising a fist to heaven rather than a receptacle, too exhausted even to hope for rescue. Then He has to remind me, once again, "Just be still!" When I finally stop thrashing about, put my cup right side up, and focus on Him, He pours.

—Hannah Abigail Peretz

I surrender to You once again, my G-d, my King, my Father. When it pleases You to answer my cries for mercy, I will be sitting still with my cup right side up and stationary.

rain

I will send down showers in season; there will be showers of blessing. —Ezekiel 34:26 (NIV)

During the early days of the pandemic shutdown, I spent a lot of time looking out my kitchen window. Watching spring's rain calmed my fears. Normally I would have been irritated by wet, gloomy weather. Instead, rain gave me hope.

Creation seemed unaffected by the uncertainty and chaos that swirled everywhere else. Rain came at just the right time, meeting the needs of flowers, grass, and trees. God cared for nature in such simple, yet important, ways.

God showed me through the rain how He showers us with similar blessings. Now, when I am anxious or uncertain, I ask God to rain His blessings upon my needs. He consistently responds by soaking my soul like a gentle spring shower.

—Brenda Yoder

Lord, rain down Your blessings upon me, providing
for all my needs. Thank You.

overcome

In this world you will have trouble. But take heart!
I have overcome the world. —John 16:33 (NIV)

The Spirit led me to the word *overcome* as my word to focus on for the year 2021. I figured the word was meant to help me overcome my difficulty in finding time to write. But I'd discover that was *not* its purpose.

At the end of 2021, as I thought over the year that had just ended, it hit me how ideal "overcome" had been. From my uncle's altered mental state while living on our property in January to his death in December. From my reaction to an immunization in the spring to my yearlong battle with a latent virus attacking my body. From my mother and our daughter's family (including an infant) rescued by boat from their flooded home to another daughter facing a broken marriage. It had certainly been a year of much to overcome.

But overcome I did . . . with God's help.

—Cathy Mayfield

*Jesus, thank You for showing me how to overcome
this world's trials with Your help.*

scrabble

Rejoice always, pray continually, give thanks in all circumstances; for this is God's will for you in Christ Jesus.
—1 Thessalonians 5:16–18 (NIV)

Lately my prayer life had been like playing Scrabble with all the vowels missing. I'd been asking God to make me more joyful, prayerful, and grateful. I never thought His answer would arrive in the form of a Scrabble board.

I discovered the red-and-black Art Deco beauty under a table at a yard sale. As soon as I saw it, it reminded me of the family who'd purchased my vintage game table when I was paring down my possessions. They couldn't wait to take it home to set up their own ongoing Scrabble game. It wasn't long before I learned the young wife who loved Scrabble had been diagnosed with cancer.

I set up my new board on a table in my living room. It prompts me to pray for my Scrabble family every time I walk by.
—Roberta Messner

I'm not just praying, Lord. I'm joyful, too, as I thank You for Your answers to those prayers!

roots

Blessed is the man who trusts in the Lord, whose trust is the Lord. He is like a tree planted by water, that sends out its roots by the stream. —Jeremiah 17:7–8 (ESV)

B rown pigtails bouncing, nose pressed to the glass, I watched the only home I knew fade away. I glanced behind me to ensure the box with my dollhouse was still perched between the car and the U-Haul.

That cross-country move when I was eight was my first time feeling uprooted. Having lived in eight different states since then, I have always longed for the roots of stability. I envied friends who went to their grandparents' house for holidays or had dozens of cousins at birthday parties.

But roots aren't found in a house, or a city, or even a person. Roots are grown when we trust in God alone to be our security. Looking back over our lives, we can trace God's faithfulness and strengthen our confidence that our roots are secure in Him—no matter what our address is.

—Bethany S. LaShell

Lord, thank You for being my security. Please grow my roots deep in the soil of Your Word.

wellness

When Jesus saw him lying there and learned that
he had been in this condition for a long time, he asked him,
"Do you want to get well?" —John 5:6 (NIV)

As I looked over the many pages of instructions from my physical therapist, I groaned. The at-home exercises were challenging and time-consuming. A few weeks before, I had tripped and fallen onto a concrete floor and dislocated my left shoulder. One doctor had recommended surgical repair, but a second doctor said he thought I could recover my strength through physical therapy. "It won't be easy," he said, "but you do want to get well, right?"

While I can't always choose physical wellness, I can choose spiritual and emotional wellness. That workout can include disciplines such as reading my Bible every day, praying, and seeking God's direction for my life in a posture of stillness. And I've found that when I am spiritually and emotionally well, the physical challenges of life won't trip me up.

—Janet Holm McHenry

*Lord God, giver of life, I seek my wellness
in personal relationship with You.*

yearn

My soul yearns for you in the night; in the morning
my spirit longs for you. —Isaiah 26:9 (NIV)

W hen I think of a newborn baby, I imagine snuggling
and rocking a sweet little bundle of joy in my arms.
However, as any parent of a newborn can testify,
when it is time to eat—watch out! That same adorable baby
craves its mother's milk with a fierce desire to survive, and
yearns for it with an intensity that must be satisfied.

In the same way, our souls yearn for God. We may not con-
sciously recognize this need, but it is there. The God who knit
us in our mother's womb designed us with a need to be loved
and to be in communion with Him. The problem is that we often get distracted by money, pleasure, and other things of this
world. These will never satisfy us the way God can. Our souls
yearn for relationship with Him.

—Mindy Baker

*Lord, help me to yearn for sweet communion with You instead
of worldly pleasures. Only You can satisfy my soul.*

closer

A man that hath friends must shew himself friendly:
and there is a friend that sticketh closer than a brother.
—Proverbs 18:24 (KJV)

When my niece was young, she enjoyed watching animated movies with me. As we settled in on the couch with popcorn and juice, she would say "closer, closer." I would oblige and scoot over nearer to her. It was never enough. She would repeat "closer." This went on until she was safely wrapped in my arms. A smile then lit up her sweet face and she would say "perfect."

Closer is a wonderful one-word prayer. That's what I want to be to Jesus. Closer. I want to rest in Him. Closer. He is my shelter. Closer. I yearn for more. Closer. I need Him to draw me safely into His arms. Closer. I can then be perfectly content in His loving presence.

—Nyla Kay Wilkerson

Lord Jesus, draw me closer to You.

sit

Then Jesus went with his disciples to a place called Gethsemane, and he said to them, "Sit here while I go over there and pray." —Matthew 26:36 (NIV)

Sometimes I have a really hard time following directions. Sit, for example. In the above verse, Jesus gives his disciples a simple command—sit and wait—and it's one that can bring spiritual benefits to anyone, no matter who or where they are. And yet I am so distracted by my to-do list and my life that I can't even accomplish this one simple task.

My hope for today is that I will have the time to simply sit and be with God. Just a few minutes of silence and stillness can have a powerful impact on my day. Jesus took the time to simply sit and be in prayer. And He commanded His disciples to do the same. Today, may we simply sit and be with God.

—Heather Jepsen

Lord, help me to simply sit and be. You call me to rest, to think, and to pray. I want to sit with You. Amen.

repaid

Although they cannot repay you, you will be repaid at the resurrection of the righteous. —Luke 14:14 (NIV)

'm often given gifts from my granddaughters, discovered when I change their diapers. And while it may be far from pleasant in the moment—requiring wet wipes and, at times, a strong stomach—these presents are, in actuality, a reminder of the joy of their presence.

Because we all know—poop happens. It's just part of life. And while poop spelled backward is, well, *poop*, diaper spelled backward is *repaid*.

That makes sense. While these little ones aren't able to offer me much more than the delight of their smiles as a reward for my love, time, and attention, the daily deposits they give are signs of their health. Yes, of their very heartbeats.

And I'd say I'm blessed—indeed, repaid in full. After all, not only do they smile up at me, but I also sense my Father smiling down— and hear Him say, "Well done, good and faithful Grandma."

—Maureen Miller

Dear Abba, sometimes I complain because life stinks. Help me count my blessings, even when they come in unique packages. Amen.

open

Yes, I am sending you to the Gentiles to open their eyes, so they may turn from darkness to light and from the power of Satan to God. —Acts 26:17–18 (NLT)

Open. *Open. Open.* I will our garage door to go up. We have a keypad outside for easy entry, but when it gets cold the door gets stubborn. And it's January in Ohio, which equals freezing. I punch our code again. The door doesn't budge. The command becomes a prayer as I shiver. "God, please open the door."

As I say the words, God reminds me there is so much more I need to ask Him to open. As I pray the word *open*, I remember them one by one: Lord, please open my heart to love the person who thinks differently than I do. Lord, please open my eyes to where You're pointing me today. Lord, please open my mind to whatever You want to teach me. Please open my hands, so I can both let go of the things I've been gripping too tightly and make room for the things You want to put there.

—Laura L. Smith

Lord, please open my heart, eyes, mind, and soul to
You and Your light. Amen.

unlikely

Please, Lord, how can I save Israel? Behold, my clan is the weakest . . . and I am the least. —Judges 6:15 (ESV)

I recently dug into my genealogy and discovered some shady characters back there. I have ancestors that were the cause of small-town scandals and others who were buried in "outcast's graves."

Many of us have family trees knotted with dysfunction and complications. Including Jesus.

Jesus's family tree includes Rahab (a harlot), David (an adulterer and murderer), and Uzziah (an arrogant ruler who openly mocked God), to name just a few. People we may consider unlikely candidates for God to use in Jesus's ancestry.

Dotted with these flawed characters, our Savior's family tree is a representation of our own. It reveals a remarkable truth that God can, will, and does use unlikely people in His divine story.

God invites us all to receive the rich love and abundant promises that turn our unlikely lives into channels of His grace.

—Kristen West

Father, please use me, such an unlikely person,
to reflect Your love and grace today!

anchor

Cast all your cares upon God; that anchor holds.
—Alfred Lord Tennyson

W e'd spent almost the entire day right off the coast of Lerwick, the largest town on the Shetland Islands. The howling winds, which were not uncommon in this corner of Great Britain, prevented our cruise ship from safely launching any tender boats bound for the nearby port. Still hopeful for a lull in the gale, we stayed anchored in one spot, longingly eyeing our destination. Unfortunately, by late afternoon our hope had faded. We weighed anchor and headed back out to sea.

Though the ship's anchor held me back from where I sorely wanted to go, ultimately it had kept me safe. I couldn't help but wonder how many times God had been an anchor in my own life, holding me back, forcing me to change the course of my plans, keeping me safe in a storm that perhaps I didn't even see.
—Vicki Kuyper

Lord, be my anchor . . . protect me, ground me,
keep me tethered closely to You. Amen.

stone

When they kept on questioning him, he straightened up and said to them, "Let any one of you who is without sin be the first to throw a stone at her." —John 8:7 (NIV)

I have an eye for detail and a precise nature. During my career as an optician, it proved vital to my work. Now that I've retired, I find it helpful for creating intricate crafts or perfecting a recipe. But when I turn a critical eye on others, it can be hurtful.

I have terrible aim and have no business throwing stones. Like Mary in the verse above, I've lived on the receiving end of stones of condemnation. Whether for my views, my emotions, or my appearance, I've felt the sting of judgment. And each time, Jesus takes my hand and rescues me.

These days I've begun collecting colorful stones in a decorative bowl, a private reminder to myself. Any "stones" I possess should be used for building up other's foundations in Christ. Judgment belongs to God.

—Heidi Gaul

Lord, keep me from throwing stones at others. Help me instead gather them to strengthen the foundations of our faith. Amen.

declare

My mouth is filled with your praise, declaring your
splendor all day long. —Psalm 71:8 (NIV)

I used to be quietly thankful, but as I've grown older, I've become more verbal with my gratitude. Psalm 71 reminds me that part of my purpose as a Christian is to ascribe to God the glory and honor due to Him. Outspoken praise is certainly part of this assignment.

One way I worship God is to praise Him aloud when I recognize His handiwork in my life: "Lord, I declare the splendor of your creative genius in the world you have made. I declare the splendor of your loving kindness in the way you invite us to have a relationship with you. I declare the splendor of your mercy that forgives all our sins."

When I do this, I point others to Him and proclaim how wonderful He is.

—Lori Hatcher

Father, help me fill Your ears with my praise as
I declare Your splendor all day long.

stubborn

I can do all things through Christ who strengthens me.
—Philippians 4:13 (NKJV)

You're stubborn enough that you can do anything you make up your mind to do." The words my father told me when I was a child lingered in my mind for years. I couldn't tell if he was criticizing me or not. After all, being called "stubborn" didn't sound like a compliment. I'd always associated the word with "stubborn as a mule," which meant hardheaded, obstinate, and uncooperative.

One day I decided to look up the word *stubborn*. It did indeed have a negative connotation, but it also had a positive one: "persistent and determined." Now *that* sounded better. I didn't mind being labeled with those words.

But the truth is, it's not my stubbornness that gives me the strength to do things. Rather, it's God's strength that matters. When He sets my course, it's His persistence—His stubbornness—that enables me to follow it.

—Marilyn Turk

Lord, thank You for enabling me to do what I do.

generosity

If you sit at a bountiful table, do not be greedy . . . remember that an evil eye is a wicked thing. —*The Book of Sirach*

In Judaism, there is the question of whether one has a "good eye" or an "evil eye." The sages described a charitable person as one with a good eye, and an "evil eye" describes a person who is greedy or lacking in charity.

I remember years ago driving with a group of friends through Vermont. I thought I had perfect vision until someone in the car let me try on their glasses. Suddenly, the lines in the center of the road went from being blurred to crystal clear.

In a similar way, I have recently come to realize that I did not have a "good eye" like I had thought—there have been times when I could have been charitable and instead made a different choice. Now, instead of making excuses for why I can't or shouldn't give, I have repented, and have begun to seek out opportunities to engage in generosity and charity.

—Dale R. Yancy

Dear Lord, forgive me for those times when I have fallen short in generosity. Incline my heart toward charity and good works. Amen.

shadow

Whoever dwells in the shelter of the Most High will rest in the shadow of the Almighty. —Psalm 91:1 (NIV)

W hy are all the young saguaro cacti growing up in the middle of a paloverde or mesquite tree?" my friend asked as he showed me photos of the lower Salt River outside of Mesa, Arizona. "Do they grow up together?"

"Baby saguaros need a nursemaid tree," I explained, "until they develop their own root system. The shadow of the tree protects them from the desert sun."

Cacti. Animals. Humans. Desert dwellers understand the importance of finding a shadow to rest under on sweltering days when temperatures soar past 100 degrees. But when circumstances get too hot for me to handle, the shading presence of the Almighty God is also somewhere I need to seek—to stretch out and rest in His shadow.

—Lynne Hartke

Dear Jesus, when my life is a real scorcher, remind me to step under Your shadow. Amen.

safe

The name of the LORD is a fortified tower; the righteous run to it and are safe. —Proverbs 18:10 (NIV)

M y husband and I tromped up Pinnacle Trail in Dorset, Vermont—an easy hike, winding up a gradual hill through a wooded area. At the top stood a solitary stone tower, about forty feet high. It looked like the ruin of an ancient castle, but we'd learned that the tower was built at the request of a Victorian woman who simply wanted an attractive estate adornment.

I walked inside the narrow doorway. The walls were thick and sturdy. I ran my hand over stones that had withstood more than a hundred years of rain, snow, and sun. I wondered if the woman long ago had ever wandered inside and felt safe and secure, as I did then. The tower may have been built for decoration, but how could anyone ignore its strength? I looked up to the heavens and pondered God, our mighty fortress, in whose protection I feel safe.

—Peggy Frezon

Lord, as I sing the old hymn, the words take on deep meaning for me: "A mighty fortress is my God, a bulwark never failing."* Amen.

*Martin Luther, "A Mighty Fortress," 1852, public domain.

masterpiece

For we are God's masterpiece. He has created us anew in Christ Jesus, so we can do the good things he planned for us long ago. —Ephesians 2:10 (NLT)

Years ago a friend led me through a visualization. She began by saying, "A famous artist is commissioned to do a sculpture of you." She then asked specific questions, beginning with, "What is the statue made of?" The exercise ended with Jesus seeing the statue, and we were left to imagine how He would react. As I visualized the scene, when Jesus saw my statue, He didn't say anything. He smiled, and I felt a deep sense of love.

My statue was of white marble, and it reminded me of pictures I had seen of Michelangelo's masterpieces, like David or the Pieta.

God is the master sculptor. Like Michelangelo, He can see the beauty in each of us. He creates through life challenges, working to free us to be the best versions of ourselves—to be living masterpieces.

—Linda Marie

Dear Lord, help us to see ourselves as You see us,
and to do the good that You have planned.

choices

I will always show you where to go. —Isaiah 58:11 (MSG)

M y friend Kim owns a Bible bookstore. When I learned she planned to set up a book table at a Christian women's conference, I offered to help. I felt proud that I'd set aside my own plans for that Saturday to help my friend.

After Kim and I arranged her products on the table, she invited me to attend the conference with her. As I worshipped with sisters in the Lord and drank in the encouraging words from each speaker, I realized with a smile how God had orchestrated this day. I thought it was my own choice to offer Kim help. But the Lord knew how empty my heart was. How much I needed this spiritual meal. He knew I'd never sign up myself—too busy—so He inspired me to help Kim. And gracious as always, He let me think it was my idea.

—Jeanette Levellie

Thank You, God, that You inspire me
to make loving choices. Amen.

voice

Then the LORD spoke to you out of the fire. You heard the sound of words but saw no form; there was only a voice.
—Deuteronomy 4:12 (NIV)

D ad's dreamy singing voice helped me find him in the big barn. I chuckled over his eclectic repertoire. As I wound my way past the hay bales and down the wooden steps, I enjoyed his concert for the cows. I grinned from the nostalgia of "Paper Doll" to the plight of the girl in "Poor Butterfly" to the lively jig of "Irishman's Shanty."

Mom's voice, on the other hand, was more trial than treat, due to surgery she had when I was in my teens. Her gravelly voice had become so different from the one I remembered soothing me with lovely lullabies when I was little.

I love the thought that in heaven, Mom's voice is beautiful again.

Dad's voice and Mom's. So different. So loved. So cherished.
—Shirley Leonard

Thanks, Lord, for the gift of music. One day we'll all be caught up in the wonder of heaven's music. The Singer. The Song. The Voice.

generations

One generation commends your works to another;
they tell of your mighty acts. —Psalm 145:4 (NIV)

Many family members know that napping children present opportunities to attack the to-do list. Once my little one closed her eyes, I scurried around the house, tackling new chores and completing unfinished tasks. The moment I decided to squeeze in one extra thing, I would spot two inquisitive eyes staring back at me.

My daughter, the silent watcher, took it all in. Many times throughout the years of her childhood I spotted her doing just that, witnessing how I managed frustrations and celebrations, observing who received my wrath and hearing who got the glory. Hopefully, she remembers more glory-giving than wrath.

Like the biblical Israelites who handed down their experiences of God's power to succeeding generations, I'm working to magnify the Lord in my family and community, hoping to pass on a spiritual legacy of faith, prayer, and praise.

—Bethanie Baker Henderson

Lord, help me to reflect Your light, to pass it on to the next generation, and to draw others to You.

uphold

Do not fear, for I am with you; Do not be afraid, for I am your God. I will strengthen you, I will also help you, I will also uphold you with My righteous right hand. —Isaiah 41:10 (NASB)

Three days after my cousin died while on a ventilator, I was admitted to the hospital for pneumonia. Fear assaulted me. Afraid of dying? No. I feared leaving my children and grandchildren. Who would help and support them if I died? Not to mention that two weeks earlier, my daughter had given birth to her first child and needed my help.

Sleep eluded me for two days while worst-case scenarios plagued my mind. Finally, I decided to pray. God reminded me that He would uphold me—and my family—in His righteous right hand. I meditated on these words. Peace replaced fear.

I rested, recovered, and, after a week in the hospital, I went home. God had upheld me, just as He promised, and I knew He would continue to do so.

—Norma Poore

Thank You, God, for giving peace when I prayed, "Father, I don't want to die and leave my family. Help me trust You even though I'm afraid."

treasure

Grant me the treasure of sublime poverty. —Francis of Assisi

Years ago, I was at a Christian writer's conference where I met a missionary on stateside leave for the first time since childhood. He lived in a remote part of western Africa, where he'd been raised from an early age. He described a simple life, devoid of most of the conveniences we all take for granted and which most of us wouldn't live without.

Over dinner, he admitted he couldn't wait to get back. He found American abundance both depressing and distracting. The relative poverty of his African life helped him treasure life, faith, and other people more. It made a big impression on me.

I've experienced both luxury and poverty and the more common middle ground between the two. I can honestly say some of the happiest times of my life were when my finances were secure but meager. I don't know that I aspire to Francis's ambition or the missionary's aim, but I've come to treasure the precious gift of detachment from wealth.

—Isabella Campolattaro

Lord, no matter my finances, help me to treasure what matters most to You.

before

Before they call I will answer; while they are still speaking I will hear. —Isaiah 65:24 (NIV)

I didn't even look up when I heard the siren. I was working on a manuscript and did not want to lose my thought before I could get it written down. I heard another siren. Then several more, all stopping close by. I snapped to attention! Smoke obscured the view out my window. I raced to the living room where my husband, Jeff, was napping. I shook him awake.

"Our pasture is on fire!"

Firefighters from four area volunteer fire departments sprayed the fast-moving flames with water from their trucks. Jeff and I fought alongside them with water hoses. We got the fire stopped at last just a hundred feet from our house. "How did you even know we had a fire?" I asked one of the firefighters.

"Some passerby called it in, I guess."

We might not always know what we need, but our Father sure does.

—Pamela Haskin

Thank You, Father, for watching over me, for taking care of me even when I am unaware of my own need.

wash

Wash me thoroughly from my iniquity, and cleanse
me from my sin. —Psalm 51:2 (NKJV)

Guilty. With splattered eggs on the neighbor's driveway, the boys' mischief was undeniable. Stunned and a bit embarrassed by the prank, we promised that our sons would not escape the repercussions of their actions. We required our boys to apologize and clean up their mess.

Cleaning involved thorough scrubbing and rinsing away the remnants of their transgression. Does that sound familiar? Isn't that what God does for you and me? The egg left behind an icky residue; that's what sin does to our lives—until God cleanses us.

The neighbors showed mercy by extending grace. God demonstrates His mercy as He purifies us from our sins. How can we receive God's cleansing? By trusting and loving God. He will give us a heart that is pure and renewed.

—Dawn Bata

*Lord, thank You for loving me enough
to wash away my sin. Amen.*

jump

*Jump, and you will find out how to unfold
your wings as you fall.* —Ray Bradbury

My childhood friend Allyson was not brave. She was afraid to drink out of the garden hose. Afraid to ride a bicycle without training wheels. She was even afraid to catch lightning bugs, convinced they would sting her. Whenever a group of neighborhood kids raked pine straw into a big pile under a tree limb so we could climb the tree and jump off into it, Allyson just stood and watched.

But one day, when she thought no one was paying attention, Allyson made her way slowly up the tree and out onto the jumping limb. There she stayed for a long time, trembling. A handful of us gathered around, not sure what to say. Finally, five-year-old Ricky piped up. "Don't think about jumping," he said. "Think about flying."

And into the pile of pine straw Allyson went. Again and again and again.

—Jennie Ivey

*Help me to be brave, Lord. And help me encourage
others to be brave too.*

ascend

I lift up my eyes to the mountains—where does
my help come from? —Psalm 121:1–2 (NIV)

The air is thin up here at 13,200 feet. Three hours ago my husband and I began our ascent of Mount Audubon. After hiking nearly four miles through the wilderness and across the alpine tundra, the summit is thirty feet ahead. We've nearly reached our goal when my husband looks back and realizes the blustery winds have kicked my vertigo into high gear. Without hesitating, he decides, "I'm calling it. Let's go down."

He sacrifices the summit to take me back to safety. For years I've battled physical limitations to explore these mountains. Modern medicine says I should probably stay on the ground. However, I've learned that sometimes ascending beyond what I believe is possible requires respecting limits and taking my time.

The same can be true of my faith walk. Sometimes I have to sacrifice my own agenda and operate within the life-giving boundaries God prescribes. As I follow His plan at His pace, He helps me ascend above every obstacle and experience His victory.

—Eryn Lynum

Dear Lord, teach me to ascend at Your pace. Amen.

content

I have learned to be content whatever
the circumstances. —Philippians 4:11 (NIV)

When I turned forty, my family went on a cruise to the Bahamas. We never got off the boat.

Our ten-year-old son, Morgan, became terribly seasick, so while passengers disembarked to explore Nassau, he asked weakly if we could watch a movie. I carried him—his gangly arms and legs wrapped around me—to the onboard theater to watch the Muppets. "Look, Mom, we have the place all to ourselves," he said.

I sighed. Watching Miss Piggy in paradise wasn't my plan. I asked God for contentment.

Morgan climbed partly onto my lap, a childlike comfort I thought he'd outgrown. He whispered, wide-eyed, that this was the fanciest theater he'd ever seen. "I hope you're having a good birthday."

I know who saw better scenery that day. But I might have made better memories.

—Laurie Davies

*Lord, even when things don't turn out the way
we hoped, help us be content. Amen.*

present

Present your bodies a living sacrifice, holy,
acceptable unto God. —Romans 12:1 (KJV)

I hosted a couple friends on a tour of a nearby national conservation area. At the entrance I presented my national park pass. The man in the entry booth took the card and asked, "What's this?" I was surprised that he didn't recognize it, but said it was a national park pass. He turned it around and showed it to me. It was the wrong card. I took it back and presented the correct card, and we were admitted.

In my daily prayers I often present my daily agenda, plans, and goals to God, which He accepts and revises according to His wisdom and will. But long ago, I presented my "whole spirit and soul and body" to God (1 Thessalonians 5:23, ESV), and I try to do so again each morning. When I present *myself* to Him, first and foremost, most other things fall into place.

—Bob Hostetler

*Lord God, I present myself to You anew—spirit,
soul, and body. Amen.*

vast

And I pray that you, . . . grasp how wide and long and high and deep is the love of Christ. —Ephesians 3:17–18 (NIV)

James's eyes filled with tears. Today had been a bad day at school.

"Matthew told me I was a bad kid," he said. What you need to know about James is that words don't bounce off him; they seep into the cracks along his soul and fester. "And I'm afraid he's right," he finished.

He and I stayed on the couch a long time that day. I told him that even if he made bad choices, he could not be a bad kid because he is one of Jesus's chosen, loved, longed-for children. "Do you know how much I love you?" I asked.

"A whole lot," he said, keeping his eyes downcast to the rug.

"You're right," I said. "Now imagine that compared to God, my love for you is like a tiny pebble, and His is a whole mountain."

James cracked a smile. That's the day that God's vast, all-consuming, ever-present love became real to him.

—Ashley Kappel

Lord, how deep and how wide is Your love for me!

eyes

The eyes of the Lord are in every place.
—Proverbs 15:3 (NKJV)

When I was a child, I marveled at my mother's ability to always know what was happening—even if she had her back turned and even sometimes when she was in another room. "Debra, stop coloring on the wall!" I'd hear her say as my crayon-laden hand was halfway to the wall.

And then I became a mother and poof! I had the blessed ability to know what my youngsters were doing—even when my back was turned. Of course, I learned it wasn't magic, but rather common sense. I do admit, though, to having a mother's sense, a God-given ability to know if my children were in danger or needed me. I'd sometimes even bolt out of a dead sleep when one of my kids needed me.

Just like a mother, God's eyes are everywhere. He never sleeps, and He never takes His eyes off His children. I know I am safe under His watch and in His care.

—Deb Kastner

God, thank You for always watching over me,
today and always.

sacrifice

Through him then let us continually offer up a sacrifice of praise to God, that is, the fruit of lips that acknowledge his name. —Hebrews 13:15 (ESV)

Sometimes God doesn't give us what we want or what we've prayed for. We get sick, we lose a job, a child runs away, our marriage falls apart—you name it. God doesn't seem to fix things the way we want, and that's when praising Him is hard. But just because we can't see His goodness doesn't mean He's forsaken us.

Offering up worship is a sacrifice during those times. But we can choose to trust God despite unanswered prayer, and trusting God's sovereignty helps us extol Him.

The scripture above says this sacrifice is to be offered "continually," whether or not God makes us happy. True adoration continues no matter the circumstance, flowing from a thankful heart. Next time you find it hard to praise Him, remember that it's not about our circumstances—it's about His worthiness.

—Tez Brooks

Father, may I never tire of honoring You. Even when I don't feel like it, I will glorify You. Amen.

unspoken

The glory of the LORD filled the house. —Ezekiel 43:5 (KJV)

I work in a public school where I can't talk about God. I'm often surprised, however, at the ways in which He is present, though His name is unspoken. My faith is strengthened each time I experience such holy moments.

They occur when a child talks about her fears, or when I see how much a child has overcome, or when kids are kind and helpful to one another—behavior sorely lacking among adults. These experiences reveal God's undeniable glory and presence.

These interactions encourage me to see that God is present in other places where His name is unspoken—hard relationships, uncomfortable situations, and other experiences where He seems absent. In these spaces, I ask God to reveal Himself in His quiet influence on the hearts of good people.

—Brenda Yoder

Lord, be present with me, though Your name is unspoken.

our

Give us each day our daily bread. —Luke 11:3 (NIV)

Now. A perfect choice for my first word-of-the-year journey, especially since it fit my plan to become a published author that year. During December my anticipation grew each time I shared my word with another person. I'd say, "Now it's my turn!"

Before January, though, another word came to mind: *our*. What kind of word is that? "Now" suited my need, my desires. "Our" fit . . . well, nothing.

Then, while relating a story about Christmas, I noticed myself saying, "My girls enjoyed the day." Aha! What about my husband's part in this? I changed it to, "Our girls enjoyed the day." It hit me that I often referred to things as mine: my daughters, my house, my dog . . . my turn. I needed to make a change. *Our* became my word of the year.

During those twelve months, I also became aware of another "our" I needed to acknowledge. What about God's part in my life?
—Cathy Mayfield

Father, what are our plans for today?

quilt

But when you give . . . do not let your left hand know what your right hand is doing. —Matthew 6:3 (NIV)

The Lone Star quilt my grandmother made has guided me for more than half a century.

Mamaw's money for extras came from what she took in at her little alteration shop. I knew her red, green, and orange polished cotton was like gold to her. But when I spotted the diamond-shaped pieces on her sewing table, I thought they were scraps, so I cut them up. A look of horror crossed her face when she saw me stitching my Barbie a skirt of many colors at her old treadle. She had just enough material for her quilt, and I'd gone and ruined everything. But Mamaw never got mad or told a soul.

Today her quilt, pieced together with pieces, graces my bed. I hear her sweet voice say: "Every day you live, Roberta, do something for someone you don't tell anyone about."

—Roberta Messner

Mamaw made peace out of pieces, Lord. I think she learned that from You.

fleece

Look, I will place a wool fleece on the threshing floor.
—Judges 6:37 (NIV)

My girlfriend and I were complete opposites in college. In spite of that, we fell in love.

Struggling emotionally with a breakup she had initiated, I knew that I needed closure. One evening I walked some distance and laid down under the branches of a stately elm tree. I prayed, "God, if you want me with this girl, then bring her to this place before the sun rises."

I awakened hours later to see her silhouette outlined in the moonlight. I blurted out, "Would you be a pastor's wife?"

She quickly replied, "Yes. I know that's what God wants." Later she would share that she had felt compelled by God to come looking for me.

We've been married and ministering together for over forty years. Putting out a fleece may be an act of faith that transforms your life.

—Rick Howerton

*Lord, I pray that the fleece I place before You today
will reveal Your will. Amen.*

afraid

When I am afraid, I put my trust in you. —Psalm 56:3 (NIV)

Monsters under the bed. Spiders and snakes. Doctor visits and shots. Children face many scary scenarios in their young lives. Some fears are legitimate, and others not so much. In the early years of grandparenting, if my grandchildren expressed fear, I sometimes told them, "Don't be afraid." Now I share a more biblical approach.

Instead of dismissing their concerns, I want to teach them how to handle them. King David, in Psalm 56, acknowledged that, regardless of our age, we all feel afraid. Instead of dismissing our feelings, he showed us what to do—bring them to God and trust Him to handle them. Then, whether our concerns are real or imaginary, we'll have brought them to the One who can do something about them.

—Lori Hatcher

Father, whenever I am afraid, help me put my trust in You.

wept

Jesus wept. —John 11:35 (NIV)

Sometimes all we can do is cry. When our hearts are breaking, our natural inclination is to let those tears flow. When those we love die, when life loses its purpose and meaning, when war strikes the nations, and when we ourselves suffer in pain, we need to let our tears out and cry. When Jesus's good friend Lazarus died, Jesus wept outside the tomb. Even our perfect Lord knew the depths of grief and sadness.

There is nothing wrong with bringing our heartache before our God. Sometimes tears are the most appropriate response to the brokenness of the world we live in. Revelation promises that God will wipe every tear from our eyes. But in the meantime, Jesus wept. We can too.

—Heather Jepsen

Lord, my heart breaks at the suffering in my own life and in our world. May my tears be an offering of my faith in You. Amen.

Jehovah

That men may know that thou, whose name alone
is Jehovah, art the most high over all the earth.
—Psalm 83:18 (KJV)

Names. We are called by many. There are proper names, nicknames, titles, and words that describe us. My dad was named Donald, but some called him Don or Donnie. He had a plethora of nicknames: Teacher, Coach, Bulldog, Hoosier, and Big D. Family called him Dad, Papaw, Uncle, Brother, Cousin, and Husband.

God also has many names. The first one we encounter in the Bible is Jehovah, meaning "I am the One who is" in Hebrew. In our Bibles, any time we read the word *Lord* in small caps, it is the English version of Jehovah. Sometimes my heart is aching, and when I pray, only that one word escapes: *Jehovah.* It is enough. I need only to call on Him, the great I Am. He is always with me, awaiting my plea for help. *Jehovah*—help me, Lord. *Jehovah*—heal me, Lord. *Jehovah*—forgive me, Lord. *Jehovah*—I love you, Lord.

—Nyla Kay Wilkerson

Jehovah, our great Lord, thank You for Your great love for us.

identity

Owning your story is the bravest thing you'll ever do.
—Brene Brown

I grew up believing my voice was too shrill, body too bony, and opinions not valid. Jesus tells me a different story. He gives us a new identity. A new narrative.

God created us in His image (Genesis 1:27). *Lord, I pray I cling to my identity as Your image-bearer.*

The Bible tells us we are fearfully—which means awe-inspiringly—and wonderfully made (Psalm 139:14). *Lord, please help me walk into a room remembering my identity in You, that You designed me wonderfully to inspire awe.*

When I have a conversation or go about my work, I pray that I own my identity as Christ's masterpiece (Ephesians 2:10). I remind myself that God put a crown on my head, and that I should feel worthy to wear it, because God says I am. I pray that I will own holiness as my identity and discard past guilt or shame Jesus has washed away (1 Peter 2:9).

—Laura L. Smith

Dear Jesus, lots of labels have been put on me, but I pray that I acknowledge and own the identity You give me. Amen.

lovingkindness

Cause me to hear Your lovingkindness in the morning, for in You do I trust; cause me to know the way in which I should walk, for I lift up my soul to You. —Psalm 143:8 (NKJV)

'd like to take fifteen extra kids to children's camp this summer," I announced in my church. "Their families don't have the money to send them. They'll need sleeping bags, personal items, and registration fees."

Following the service, a man approached me, checkbook in hand. "How much do you need—for all fifteen?"

Now, after many years in children's ministry, I can't recall the amount of the gift or even the man's name. But I will never forget his kindness, motivated by a God-inspired love for kids in need. His caring act of "lovingkindness" still stirs my heart to this day.

I know that God is "loving" and full of "kindness" too. Neither word alone fully captures His caring character. When the two words are combined, however, a gentle picture emerges— one of lovingkindness—a kindness motivated by His love for me.

—Becky Alexander

Dear God, I bask in Your lovingkindness today. Amen.

pilgrimage

Blessed are those whose strength is in you, whose hearts are set on pilgrimage. —Psalm 84:5 (NIV)

As I walked along the Via Dolorosa, I couldn't help but wonder if Jesus's feet had once touched the same stone as mine, on the day he traveled this street toward his death on the cross. Although the narrow alleyway in Jerusalem's Old City was chaotic, packed shoulder-to-shoulder with tourists, vendors, and locals, I was overwhelmed by a quiet sense of the sacred. I felt close to God.

But a pilgrimage to Israel isn't a secret passage into God's presence. Every day I'm on a journey that leads me either closer to or farther away from Him. Every decision I make, every action I take, every word I say is a step, leading me one direction or the other. *Pilgrimage* is a one-word prayer that reminds me life is a journey. I never remain in the same place, even if I never leave home. Where will life's pilgrimage lead me today?

—Vicki Kuyper

Lord, I pray today's pilgrimage will lead me ever closer to You. Amen.

new

Therefore, if anyone is in Christ, the new creation has come: The old has gone, the new is here! —2 Corinthians 5:17 (NIV)

Scoring items at thrift shops is one of my favorite pastimes. As a result, many of my possessions might seem a little worn or damaged—just like me.

As a child, instead of receiving consistent spiritual guidance, I was given new clothes and toys. Those material gifts were offered with the best intentions, but when I reached adulthood, I was left feeling empty, wanting something more. Then . . . Jesus.

Today I stand at the thrift shop's register in my secondhand clothes, grateful that the most valuable item I possess—the only one that matters—is the one I've had for years. It will never grow old. It's my eternal spirit. Because I am in Christ, I am always a new creation. The old is gone. Amen.

—Heidi Gaul

Jesus, thank You for refreshing my soul every morning, and making me new in You. Amen.

doing

Jesus said, "Father, forgive them, for they do not know what they are doing." —Luke 23:34 (NIV)

Last week I invited a friend over for supper and a time of fun fellowship. A half hour after she was to have arrived, I called and messaged her. She had totally forgotten! Ouch! And I prayed, "Father, forgive her, for she totally does not know how badly she hurt me."

I am so thankful for Jesus giving me an example to follow when it comes to forgiving someone who has hurt me. I aim to make this prayer my response any time I feel hurt by another person. It truly helps to take away the sting of the hurt.

I know that most of the time, people are not out to hurt me. They are human and frail, just like I am. And I pray people can forgive me when I hurt them, because sometimes I, too, don't know what I'm doing.

—Sharon J. Morris

Dear Jesus, thank You for forgiving Your persecutors while You were on the cross and for showing us how we can forgive others. Amen.

fingerprints

Bind them on your fingers; write them on the tablet of your heart. —Proverbs 7:3 (NIV)

A s a grandparent, I've seen my share of fingerprints left by grandkids all throughout the house. They've even left their fingerprints forever etched in my concrete sidewalk and patio. When I see those fingerprints embedded in concrete, it's a reminder that they've been here, having lived with us for a year while their father was serving in the Middle East.

The Bible tells us that God has left His fingerprints throughout the heavens as well as our lives. The first of the wonderful saints whom God has brought into my life was a neighbor who my parents hardly knew. She knocked on our door, asking permission to take me and my younger brother to her church for Sunday school. I can't even remember her name, but she was one of the first fingerprints of God in my life.

I'm so thankful for fingerprints, especially the ones that have been left by God.

—Dale R. Yancy

Lord, when I look back, I see Your fingerprints all throughout my life.

look

My ears had heard of you but now my eyes
have seen you. —Job 42:5 (NIV)

"Look!" I said, as I tried to get my grandchildren's undivided attention. "Over here." I snapped my fingers as I attempted to get a photo while they posed on a piece of playground equipment. At ages ten, eight, five, and three, they were easily distracted. The oldest boy balanced on top of the monkey bars while his younger brother hid under the slide. The oldest girl frowned, not wanting to be in the picture at all, while the youngest one played with the stones at her feet. Their attention was everywhere but where I wanted it to be—on me.

But I must admit I am equally preoccupied when God wants my attention. "Look," He says in the beautiful colors of a sunrise. "Look again," through the kindness of a friend. "Look," as He meets my daily needs. "Look," as He answers my prayers for wisdom and guidance. "Look."

—Lynne Hartke

Jesus, let me focus my eyes on You and look. Amen.

companion

So do not fear, for I am with you; do not be dismayed, for I am your God. I will strengthen you and help you; I will uphold you with my righteous right hand. —Isaiah 41:10 (NIV)

There are times when life feels like an extremely bad, low-budget movie with stale popcorn. In seasons of loneliness and despair, God can seem not so close.

After escaping a very toxic relationship, I did not have an address to call my own for nearly a year. There were times the address was whatever parking lot I landed in.

Then there was my red-dappled wiener dog, Josiepuppy. When God did not seem near, Josie did not judge. She was just the companion I needed in those dark, uncertain times.

Have you ever noticed that *dog* is *God* spelled backward? Alone as I was, I was never really alone. I read an article some years ago saying that a pet is God's way of showing us His unconditional love. Could it be that God sent Josiepuppy in His place?

—Cynthia Rhue

Lord, help us to see you in Your varied outfits and know that You are closer than we think. Amen.

attend

Attend to my words; incline thine ear unto my sayings.
—Proverbs 4:20 (KJV)

'm reading a book about listening to God in quiet meditation. I love reading the book. But practicing the discipline of
sitting quietly in God's presence? Sigh. My usual method is to
pace and pray. When I'm still, my mind spins to solve a problem, go over the items on my to-do list, and even ponder what
to cook for dinner (Really? I'm not a fan of cooking).

A few days ago, after I yakked all the way through my time
with God, I heard Him whisper, "That was a great conversation,
Jeanette."

I sensed His sarcasm. "Okay, Lord, I'll sit and do my best to
listen. But You know I stink at this."

"Jeanette, don't try so hard. It's not up to you to make this
happen. That's My job." Aha. I sat. And He spoke.

—Jeanette Levellie

Lord, show me how to attend to Your words
and listen to You better. Amen.

lonely

Let your conduct be without covetousness; be content with such things as you have. For He Himself has said, "I will never leave you nor forsake you." —Hebrews 13:5 (NKJV)

I recently bemoaned being single. I felt alone and wished I had someone to share my life with.

I felt God whisper, "You have Me."

"I want a human with skin. You need arms to give a hug," I complained. "How come my friends have husbands and children, but not me?"

"My plans for you are good. You can choose not to covet their lives and be content. Fix your eyes on Me. I will always be with you and cherish you forever. I hold you in the palm of my hand."

I felt the Lord's love wash over me anew. My heart rested in His embrace and the loneliness fled.

Maybe you have felt lonely sometimes. If so, know you are never alone or unloved. He will never leave you nor forsake you.

—Joanna Eccles

Dear Lord, please be near the lonely and let Your love saturate their souls. Amen.

undisturbedness

He who dwells in the shelter of the Most High will remain secure. —Psalm 91:1 (AMP)

When my nerves could no longer deal with the constant activity of our five young children, I recalled a story about the mother of John Wesley, one of the founders of Methodism. Susanna Wesley was the mother of nineteen children, ten of whom survived infancy. It is said that she daily set aside a prescribed quiet time for herself. Throwing her apron up over her own face and head, she spent a few minutes alone with God. Her children knew to withdraw and hush, making it possible for her to have prayer times.

I learned from her that even in the midst of a daily hurricane of family and children, it is possible to find a quiet place to gather your own thoughts and speak to God. For my quiet time, I got up at four in the morning for my devotions and laundry. Usually I only managed this twice a week, which was just enough respite for my soul to remain "secure."

—Judy MacMillan

Thank You, God, for giving us the ability to find You and Your secret place, no matter when or how.

myopic

Be Thou my vision, O Lord of my heart. —Eleanor H. Hull

For the last forty years I have needed corrective eye lenses. I have trouble seeing in the distance, and without my glasses I cannot clearly distinguish between threats and pleasantries. I have walked out in front of traveling cars and have also missed well-wishes from neighbors.

Sometimes I wonder if I am also spiritually myopic. The shortsightedness of sin blinds me to the needs of others and keeps me in a state of self-centeredness. Being spiritually near-sighted, I cannot see what lies on the horizon and cannot trust my limited vision to stay out of situations that might lead me down the wrong path.

Fortunately, God is a vision maker: He corrects my spiritual eyesight so that when I listen to His instruction, follow His correction, and entrust my care to Him, I can see as He wants me to. I may see things dimly now, but with God I eventually will see 20/20.

—Virginia Ruth

All-Seeing God, may my myopia remind me to seek Your daily correction and to see the world as You see it. Amen.

tend

The lamps on the pure gold lampstand before the
LORD must be tended continually. —Leviticus 24:4 (NIV)

This week has been frantic, with my kids in daily play rehearsals and me out most nights presenting at churches. Our interactions have been reduced to quick hugs in passing and text messages to stay connected. My heart aches to tend to them: to sit, without distraction, and listen to what's on their hearts and minds; to cook them meals and play silly games to fill their bellies and lighten their souls. I can't wait for next week, when we'll have more than five minutes together.

Likewise, I know Jesus yearns to tend to me. In the midst of my chaos, I can imagine him waiting to sit with me, without distraction, and listen to what's on my heart and mind; to shower me with grace to fill my heart and lighten my spirit. Although He can do that in just five minutes, I long to make more time together so that He can further tend to my soul.

—Claire McGarry

*Great Tender of Hearts, remind me to spend more time
at Your feet so You can tend to my soul. Amen.*

rumpus

Be still, and know that I am God. —Psalm 46:10 (NIV)

My boys loved the book *Where the Wild Things Are*. In the book, the main character, Max, sails to a land with Wild Things, who make him their king. He orders, "Let the wild rumpus start!" When it gets crazy, he declares, "Now STOP!" and tames them.

While listening to the story of Jesus calming the storm, my five-year-old pointed to an image of Jesus, saying, "STOP! Be still!" with His hand outstretched. Excitedly, my son said, "That's just like Max! Is Jesus in the Wild Things story too? Are they friends?"

While we clearly have work to do differentiating fact and fiction, this childlike correlation makes me laugh. I enjoy thinking of Jesus stepping into my life (which is often in full "rumpus mode") and taming it. I love to picture Jesus with the children He loved—like my very own Wild Things—stooping down with a twinkle in His eye, and whispering, "Now . . . let the wild rumpus start!"

—Sarah Greek

Let my day run wild with laughter and peace in equal measure, and with security knowing that my King has it all in His hands.

ignore

I don't have to attend every argument I'm invited to.
—W. C. Fields

My late mother used to say that I'd rather argue than eat. She was right, though I preferred the term "debate." In today's contentious times, it seems that plenty of folks are just like I was. On TV, on call-in shows on the radio, and especially on social media, perfect strangers feel free to argue with people they don't know and will likely never meet.

I used to join these word battles, but not anymore. When something angry or negative, true or not, is being said or written, I choose to opt out. I close my mouth or take my fingers off the keyboard. I walk away. I've come to understand that the most helpful—and holy—thing I can do for myself and others is to ignore arguments and to strive for understanding.

—Jennie Ivey

Heavenly Father, may I seek to follow the path of peace.

sift

What has straw in common with wheat? declares the Lord.
—Jeremiah 23:28 (ESV)

My four-year-old daughter sits on the lake's shore. Her big brothers splash in the water as she busies herself with countless crystalized grains. Her small hands dump heaps of sand into a flat plastic sifter. The grains slide side-to-side as she shakes the sieve until they find a vacant hole to fall through, revealing beach treasures of pebbles, small sticks, and bird feathers for her to inspect. It is a careful operation and demands her attention for quite some time, like a prospector after gold.

I sense God doing similar work in my soul. Like my daughter's rhythmic motions, He is gentle with my heart, parting futile straw from valuable wheat. I'm learning to embrace this work. Like King David in Psalm 139:23 (ESV), I pray, "Search me, O God, and know my heart! Try me and know my thoughts!" He sifts my thoughts, ideas, and dreams, letting the temporal fall to the ground while extracting what holds eternal value.

—Eryn Lynum

Dear Lord, sift my thoughts each morning. Winnow out the straw and chaff and employ what is good and useful for Your kingdom.

compete

If you have raced with men on foot and they have worn you out, how can you compete with horses?
—Jeremiah 12:5 (NIV)

I felt deficient in my early Christian life because I didn't have a "life verse." Was I absent when God handed them out? Having a life verse felt like a Christian rite of passage that I had missed.

And then I read Jeremiah 12:5.

Just that morning I had been lamenting a series of unjust attacks. *How long will this go on?* I cried out to God. I wanted my adversary to relent.

The Old Testament prophet Jeremiah had a much harder job. He grew weary from trying to pull an entire kingdom into line. But I sensed that God said to Jeremiah what he was saying to me too: "Stop letting people make you tired. I want you to run with horses!" And, voila, I had my life verse. Since then, I've tried to compete only in the races God wants me to run.

What races are you competing in?

—Laurie Davies

*Lord, when I'm tempted to focus on earthly battles,
equip me for heavenly victories. Amen.*

plunge

Plunge into the sublime seas, dive deep, and swim far.
—Ralph Waldo Emerson

M y fourteen-year-old grandson takes a swim class in his high school. He recently told me that the others in his class dip their toes in the pool and always report that the water is cold. They dread getting into the water, shivering the whole time. He, however, plunges right in, diving deep and letting the water, however warm or cold it may be, invigorate him.

I told him that I love his approach. It's how I aspire to live my life. I want to plunge into my day, whatever it may hold, with the knowledge that God loves me, the faith that He is in control, and the hope that He will help me to dive deep and swim far, whatever challenges I may face. Since that conversation with my grandson, I've taken to praying the word *plunge*, especially in the mornings.

—Bob Hostetler

*Great God, my Father, let me plunge into this day,
dive deep, and swim far. Amen.*

gentle

A gentle answer turns away wrath, but a harsh
word stirs up anger. —Proverbs 15:1 (NIV)

Both arms loaded with brand-name clothes, I deposited them on the counter at the register. The young woman there was abrupt when she informed me she was closed, and that I had to take it to another register. My first thought was to tell her off and leave the clothes where they were. Next, I thought about asking to speak to her manager. But then the Spirit came on me and I responded, "It sounds like you're angry. What's going on?"

In tears, she said the school had called to come pick up her sick son. Her supervisor refused to give her time off, and she didn't know what to do.

Though I may have felt as if I had every right to be angry, taking the time to find gentle words turned away her wrath and changed the whole scene.

—Les Burnette

*Father, please help me look past anger and respond
in gentleness. In Jesus's name, amen.*

unexpected

And I am certain that God, who began the good work within you, will continue his work until it is finally finished on the day when Christ Jesus returns. —Philippians 1:6 (NLT)

M y husband and I were clearing out last year's pots, getting them ready for new spring plants. I found a few tiny volunteers that had survived the winter. I couldn't bear to toss them in the yard debris bin, so I replanted them in a rectangular planter designed to sit atop the deck railing.

To be honest, that planter looked pretty pitiful at first. I wondered if I should have just tossed them after all. My initial expectations were low, but I decided to trust that our God is bigger than my expectations.

Imagine my delight when God accomplished the unexpected with my rescued misfits. By early summer, cute daisies and yellow snapdragons burst forth, and purple and white alyssum cascaded over the side. That planter was the highlight of our deck all summer long and into the fall.

—Linda L. Kruschke

Lord of all Creation, thank You for the unexpected blessings You bestow on Your people. Amen.

scars

He showed them his hands and side. The disciples were overjoyed when they saw the Lord. —John 20:20 (NIV)

B eing a trauma survivor has left me with scars etched on my heart, mind, and emotions. Surviving insecurity, anxiety, a miscarriage, and the suicides of my son and husband have taught me that scars can tell a story that testify of God's greatness and, thus, can be beautiful. Jesus's scars proved His identity and validated His story—Jesus was who He said He was, the son of God.

I've discovered that as I continuously surrender all to my Lord, giving myself over to God's plans and purpose for life, healing comes to festering wounds. As God writes new chapters to my life and changes my perception, the scars become a permanent memorial to the wondrous work He does. He creates beauty from the devastation.

—Manette Kay

Father God, thank You for the scars Jesus endured for me. Please take my broken heart and accept my scars as an offering of gratitude for the forgiveness and mercy You have given me. Amen.

reminder

Ritual is not a path; ritual is the reminder that there is a path.
—Unknown

Every Friday night a reminder to light the Sabbath candles appears on my calendar. I never actually light them; I stopped doing that years ago, after my cat set his big, fluffy tail on fire by leaping onto the high counter where the candles stood before I could head him off.

Some Jews who are more observant than I am might think not lighting Shabbat candles is a bad thing. But for me, the reminder is enough to accomplish what the candles are supposed to do: draw awareness to the sacredness of the Sabbath and to God's foremost presence during that time. I need reminding when the week has been particularly hard for any number of reasons, distracting me from the purpose of a time of rest and worship. That purpose—making me aware of my need to take a step back and focus—is apparent at once when I look at the calendar. And my cat is safe from flames.

—Rhoda Blecker

The candles might get people's attention, Lord, but it's the message that is important. Thank You for all that You teach me.

marvelous

So thank GOD for his marvelous love. —Psalm 107:8 (MSG)

I love old words. Words that have been lost in the yesterdays. Words that roll off the tongue. *Serendipitous. Kaleidoscopic. Delightful.* And the word *marvelous.*

Our daughters would fuss when I used my "big words," as they called them. But today's words lack the marvelous essence of the words of days gone by. When visiting a butterfly house, we had the delightful experience of watching one land on our infant grandson. I considered it serendipitous, a tiny miracle God gave us. And with all the colors of the flitting butterflies and foliage filling the room, it felt like looking through a child's toy—kaleidoscopic.

As I chose a verse for this devotion, God delighted me with another of my favorite linguistic treats—alliteration: "So, thank God for His marvelous love, for His miracle mercy to the children He loves." How marvelously serendipitous of Him!

—Cathy Mayfield

Marvelous Majesty, let me always delight myself in
You and Your marvelous love.

picture

God has said, "Never will I leave you; never will
I forsake you." —Hebrews 13:5 (NIV)

Facial tumors had left me with nerve damage—a lopsided
smile and a left eye that didn't do what I wanted it to do.
So when folks snapped pictures of me, I usually managed
to destroy them.

I recently flipped through a friend's old photo album.
"Where'd these come from?" I asked. I thought I'd torn any
pictures of me into shreds, but here were three dreadful ones.
I studied an image of me after a big tumor surgery; another
when my face was a road map of incisions; one when a mouth
tumor made my cheek bulge. Yet I wasn't repulsed at those
pictures as in times past. A closer look revealed so much more
than Roberta. The woman in the photos had an otherworldly
I'll-get-through-this strength I'd never noticed before. Those
pictures didn't just show me; they showed the One who stood
beside me through all of it.

—Roberta Messner

May there never be a picture of me without You, Lord.

grip

For I, the LORD your God, hold your right hand; it is I who say to you, "Do not fear, I will help you." —Isaiah 41:13 (NRSVUE)

I grew up in a small town without much traffic and only one main highway. But when we found ourselves in any kind of parking lot or with a street to cross, my father would stretch out his arm and grip my hand. He scanned the traffic and took stock of any dangers. I immediately felt safe and secure with my hand in his grip because he was on the job.

There are times now, as an adult, when I long for the safety I felt with my father gripping my hand. At those times I remind myself that God is also on the job. He is gripping my hand, and Jesus promises that nothing and no one can dare snatch me out of that grip.

—Mary Hix

Abba Father, help me to look for reminders that You are on the job and I am safely in Your grip. Amen.

zen

You will keep in perfect peace those whose minds are steadfast, because they trust in you. —Isaiah 26:3 (NIV)

Between the hours of five and seven each evening, our house is taken over by general mayhem. Everyone is home, everyone is tired, everyone is hungry. They need me for everything—comfort after a long day, dinner for their tummies, and help on their homework—and unfortunately, I need every part of me to accomplish each of their tasks!

I read once that when babies are fussy, take them outside or to the water. We adhered to that almost religiously—long baths in the winter, pool afternoons in the summer. Now I find that soothing, calm praise music, played quietly on our network of smart devices, resets the house from a roaring den of needs to a zen space filled (mostly) with kind words and eager readers.

Maybe your zen space is journaling, or perhaps it's exercise with friends. Whatever it is, find it today and allow your centered soul to breathe light into those around you.

—Ashley Kappel

Lord, help me find my zen space so that I may see and hear You more clearly.

hard

Ah, Lord God! It is you who have made the heavens and the earth by your great power and by your outstretched arm! Nothing is too hard for you. —Jeremiah 32:17 (ESV)

Are there people on your prayer list who are easy to pray for? You love them so much and the prayers just flow from your mouth to God's ears with ease. You pray for everything that concerns them. Because you care so deeply for them, words come easily.

Then there are others you start to pray for and it's hard. It's a struggle. Hard because they've hurt someone you love. Hard because they've treated you unkindly. It's hard to pray; the words get stuck in your throat. It's so hard that tears fall, but you finally pray: *Bless this one*, and *may Your will be done. Do what's best for them.*

You didn't want to pray for them, but you did. You feel at peace.

—Donna Collins Tinsley

Lord, help us to truly love those who are hard to pray for. May You guide them to become people who are easy to pray for.

audience

The whole world sought audience with Solomon to hear the wisdom God had put in his heart. —1 Kings 10:24 (NIV)

From peasants to kings, people across the globe desired to visit with Solomon, the wisest man who ever lived. People knew time with Solomon would benefit them, for individuals become like those with whom they associate.

Peter and John understood this more than anyone. In fact, Acts 4:13 reveals that the Sanhedrin who were questioning them were astonished by the level of power and authority displayed by the disciples in spite of their uneducated background. The religious leaders knew it was because Peter and John had audience with Jesus for three years.

Sadly, I pursue time with my television or social media rather than my Savior. I digress with hours spent under the world's influence. But when I seek audience with Christ, I become bolder and more confident in sharing my faith with others. This gives Him the opportunity to transform me.

—Tez Brooks

Lord, may I seek audience with You every day that
I might be altered into Your image. Amen.

raise

The LORD said to Abram, after Lot had separated from him, "Raise your eyes now, and look from the place where you are, northward and southward and eastward and westward." —Genesis 13:14 (NRSVUE)

I plodded into the kitchen in my bathrobe and slippers, stood at the sink, and stared down at the dirty dishes—pots and pans smeared with caked-on spaghetti sauce. I could have done the dishes last night, but nooo, I decided I'd do it tomorrow. Well, now it was tomorrow.

Just then I happened to raise my eyes. I looked out the kitchen window, and there was the morning sun peeking over the horizon, painting the sky a Wheaties-box orange. It was a glorious sight, and it had been there the whole time. All I had to do was raise my eyes. Feeling renewed, I gave those pots and pans the cleaning of their life.

What a good word to pray—*raise*. Now I find myself asking God to raise my vision to see the beauty of life, to raise my heart when I am downcast, and to raise my confidence in the promises of His Word.

—Lou Lotz

Father, raise my vision, my heart, my hopes. Amen.

protection

But let all who take refuge in you be glad; let them ever sing for joy. Spread your protection over them, that those who love your name may rejoice in you. —Psalm 5:11 (NIV)

I walk to the window and wave to my daughter as she pulls out of the driveway. *God, please protect her.* I pray this same prayer whenever one of my four kids leaves the house—for God to protect them when I have zero control of their safety.

My kids need God's protection. But so do I. I need protection from things I'll hear and see and experience that distract me from God and His promises. *God, please protect me and my heart.*

People all around the world need God's protection. The news tells me of innocent people being attacked. *Lord, please protect them.*

I'm so grateful God is bigger and stronger than you and me, greater and more powerful than we can imagine. We don't have the capacity to keep everyone safe, but God does. I'm so thankful for His protection.

—Laura L. Smith

There are so many fragile and dangerous things in this broken world, Lord, but You are our Protector. I pray for Your protection. Amen.

impossible

But Jesus looked at them and said, "With man this is impossible, but with God all things are possible." —Matthew 19:26 (ESV)

We recently received a call saying our guests, whom we'd expected in two hours, would arrive in fifteen minutes. No amount of Southern cooking or quiet sips (or guzzles) of coffee could remedy what felt impossible in my heart—to be the hostess God desired. While I enjoy welcoming people to our home, I admittedly struggle with extended overnight stays.

With the fifteen-minute countdown underway, I prayed: *Lord, help me be who I can't possibly be without You.* Immediately, the heaviness lifted, making way for an undercurrent of peace to flow through my heart and mind. That peace allowed me to focus on what was important, and to accept that what I could accomplish in fifteen minutes would be enough.

Yes, God can move mountains, but He also longs to make the impossible possible in our everyday lives.

—Cathy Baker

Lord, thank You for making all things possible for our good and for Your glory. Amen.

beckon

Come to me, all you who are weary and burdened,
and I will give you rest. —Matthew 11:28 (NIV)

O ne night I was going through my usual routine. Check the doors, let the dog out, round up the cats. When I called for the cats, Stella came quickly, but where was Luna? I called again, I searched inside and out, I shook the treat bag—that usually did the trick. Still no Luna. Finally, I had to admit that somehow she had escaped our screened-in porch.

So the kids and I took our search outside the safety of the porch. Finally, we found her on top of the screen enclosure, meowing pitifully, just out of our reach. To get her to come down, we beckoned, we bribed, and finally I got a stepstool and cajoled her to come just a little closer. When she finally overcame her fear, she stepped into my arms. Safe and sound.

God beckons us to come. He calls us. He woos us. He wants us to be safe in His care.

—Stephanie Reeves

Father God, thank You for Your great love for me that will search me out, and find me, and give me rest. Amen.

decisions

Going at once to Jesus, Judas said, "Rabbi!"
and kissed him. —Mark 14:45 (NIV)

I face decisions all day, every day. Will breakfast be yogurt or a slice—or even two—of cold pizza? Will I rise early for quiet time with the Lord or choose to sleep in? Will I confront the individual that slighted me or forgive her and move on?

Judas Iscariot's kiss, which marked Jesus for death, wasn't his first bad decision. With all sorts of options, he sealed his fate one bad choice at a time, such as the time he helped himself to the contents of the disciples' money bag (John 12:6).

Because one simple decision often leads to an entire series of choices, today I'll choose the healthy meal and savor my moments with Jesus. I'll release the resentment that holds no place in my life. I'll choose to follow His lead. One choice at a time.

—Heidi Gaul

Lord, empower me to make choices that will bless
You and the people I meet today. Amen.

broken

He heals the brokenhearted and binds up their wounds.
—Psalm 147:3 (NIV)

W e can't get rid of it. It's a chipped and broken piece of pottery that my daughter made as a child. She shaped it (as well as her tiny hands could) to resemble her, with two arms, two legs, a torso, a head, and long, unruly hair. At first, only one arm broke. Then a leg. And so on, until now only the torso and head remain. But my wife and I treasure it. It's broken, yes, but it's beautiful to us.

Maybe you've heard of *kintsugi*, the Japanese art of repairing broken pottery by mending the areas of breakage with gold dust mixed into lacquer. It highlights the brokenness, making the object even more beautiful than before . . . *because* it was broken. God does that with us. He is doing it right now. However cracked or crushed we may feel, He uses our brokenness to heal, help, and beautify.

—Bob Hostetler

Lord, pour Your beauty into my broken places. Amen.

purify

If we confess our sins, he is faithful and just and will
forgive us our sins and purify us from all unrighteousness.
—1 John 1:9 (NIV)

We live in a neighborhood serviced by a water company that's notorious for not maintaining the pipe system that carries clean water to our homes. Last summer we received seven boil water advisories. After each pipe repair, they instructed us to boil the water we used for drinking, cooking, and brushing our teeth. The heat would purify it and remove any bacteria or contaminants that could make us sick.

First John 1:9 tells us if we confess our sins, God will forgive and purify us from all unrighteousness. When I confess, I invite God to purify my mind and help me think only those thoughts that honor Him. To purify my heart and help me follow Him wholeheartedly. To purify my actions that I might point others to Him and bring Him joy.

—Lori Hatcher

*Father, purify me from all unrighteousness. Make me
more like Your Son and my Savior, Jesus.*

unceasing

Pray without ceasing. —1 Thessalonians 5:17 (KJV)

B ecause I've been in church choirs since I was small, I have a huge memory collection of anthems and hymns. When reading the Bible, I often come across text that was used as a lyric in one of those songs. I wind up singing that song to myself, and then it gets stuck in my head, playing on repeat until it almost drives me crazy. There's even a term for this phenomenon: *earworm.*

I began to wonder, though, if those earworms might actually be good for me. If I sing the same spiritual song over and over, couldn't that be considered unceasing prayer? The words of those songs certainly keep my mind on God. Now I pay attention to what I'm singing, using the words as a prayer, and that earworm becomes a blessing!

—Kim Sheard

Lord, help me to pray without ceasing, and to keep my mind on You. Amen.

mercies

Through the LORD's mercies we are not consumed, because
His compassions fail not. They are new every morning;
great is Your faithfulness. —Lamentations 3:22–23 (NKJV)

I n the Amidah ("The Standing Prayer"), the eighteenth
blessing is thanksgiving for God's unfailing mercies.

Yesterday I was reminded of this ancient blessing when
my daughter dropped her three young children off at preschool. On the way home, for some unknown reason, the rear
side window imploded, sending jagged shards of glass into
the interior of the back seat. Just a few minutes earlier, her son,
Jack, had been strapped in his car seat next to that window. He
and his two-year-old sister, who was next to him in her own car
seat, would have been in the direct path of that flying glass.

Some would call it "luck," but I know God's unfailing mercy
protected my grandchildren from severe injury or even death.
I thank God for His tender, unfailing mercies, which are new
every morning.

—Dale R. Yancy

*Dear Lord, thank You for Your unfailing love
and Your tender mercies. Amen.*

sign

You make known to me the path of life. —Psalm 16:11 (ESV)

Rattlesnakes Only Beyond This Point."

The sign at the edge of the trail at the Boyce Thompson Arboretum near Superior, Arizona, got my attention. After hours spent meandering the different desert loops, I had been tempted to investigate the shaded riparian area off the trail. I could hear the cool, enticing stream just beyond my reach, where flickers, cactus wrens, and towhees twittered and chirped.

The thought of snakes stopped me, reluctantly. I appreciated the sign's clever wording. Rather than posting a "Stay on the Trail or Stay Home" sign, the staff had chosen a positive spin to encourage visitors like me to exhibit caution. In my walk of faith, my tendency to ignore the Spirit's gentle nudging and to wander off on faith-rattling shortcuts hadn't served me well in the past either.

I obeyed the sign.

—Lynne Hartke

Jesus, prompt me to follow Your nudges and signs today and not to stray from Your path of life. Amen.

known

But whoever loves God is known by God.
—1 Corinthians 8:3 (NIV)

I woke up feeling under the weather, and I certainly didn't look like myself. My eyes were red, my face pale, and my hair a mess. But when I turned on my computer, the software recognition program had no problem recognizing me. It blipped right on, ready to work.

In the Bible there were many times when the people didn't recognize Jesus. The disciples on the boat didn't recognize him walking on the water. Mary Magdalene didn't recognize him in the tomb. But God always recognizes us. He sees us when we are healthy or ill. He sees us when we are at our best and worst. Best of all, He knows us, down to the very hairs on our head.

Despite not feeling well, I smiled at the thought that Jesus recognizes me, in every detail. What a blessing to be so known!

—Peggy Frezon

Father, You know me. You know my desires and my weaknesses.
You know where I will succeed. You know what is best for me.
I can trust You because I am known.

focus

But seek first the kingdom of God and his righteousness,
and all these things will be provided for you.
—Matthew 6:33 (CSB)

There's always a clue that shows me when I've lost focus on my work. I head straight for the kitchen. I find myself rummaging through the cabinets looking for a snack. It has nothing to do with hunger and everything to do with giving up when it feels hard to focus.

The problem is that I've yet to find a snack that helps me focus. So often we feel something (like a lack of focus) and start rummaging around in the cabinets for a solution. But there is no solution in the cabinet. The solution we needed was there all along.

When we lose focus and need to find our way back, God promises to guide us to that which is best for us. Our only job is to put our focus back on Him.

—Rebecca Hastings

Father, help me focus on You before anything else.
I trust You will show me what I need to do and give me
the strength to do it. Amen.

visualize

Therefore I say to you, whatever things you ask when you pray, believe that you receive them, and you will have them. —Mark 11:24 (NKJV)

M y friend Nanette told me about a distinctive way to pray. "Ask God for what you know His will is, and then visualize that answer." I'd successfully prayed this way before, based on Norman Vincent Peale's book *Imaging*. I closed my eyes to pray and imagined my daughter's face glowing with joy after landing a great job.

But Nanette's third step tripped me up. "After doing that, let God grant your request in His own way."

What? Don't give God ideas for seven possible ways to answer my prayer? Don't worry about my daughter's lack of marketable skills? What a unique concept. Let God answer my prayers in His own way. When I tried Nanette's suggestion, the Lord flooded my heart with His peace. But of course. He's smarter than I am.

—Jeanette Levellie

*Dear Lord, I invite You to answer my prayers
in Your unique ways. Amen.*

feel

Be kind and compassionate to one another.
—Ephesians 4:32 (NIV)

She sat on the curb, crying inconsolably. Her shopping cart, overturned. A bottle, broken. Her liquid companion pooling into the gutter. I was already late for work as the sun prematurely baked the sidewalk on this early Southern California morning. But I couldn't leave her there in such a bitterly sad state. I approached slowly, gently, and crouched beside her.

Her breath was sour with alcohol and tears. Sobbing as if her best friend had died, she rocked back and forth, mourning its evaporating spirit. Suddenly time stood still—long enough for me to feel. I rested my hand on her back and said the only words valid in this crazy world: "God loves you so much."

Then . . . silence. She turned, and her bloodshot eyes softened. "I know He does," she said. "I just needed to hear it again."

—Kimberly Shumate

Father, how fragile we all are in a world without compassion. I pray that I feel more today.

unafraid

For God hath not given us the spirit of fear; but of power, and of love, and of a sound mind. —2 Timothy 1:7 (KJV)

After a fierce windstorm, I noticed a large black object in the field behind my house. It resembled a tarp, but the one on my pickup was intact. I should have investigated, but I was afraid: what if it was something dangerous?

A couple of days later, my son Patrick walked out, took a look, and laughed. "It's a trampoline bed!" he said. "A new one." The object that had provoked so much anxiety was something harmless, something designed for fun.

None of my neighbors owned a trampoline, so it's on a shelf in my garage waiting to be claimed. In the meantime it reminds me that irrational fears of the unknown are just that. Irrational. So when I'm confronted with an object or situation that is a bit scary, I say the word *unafraid*. I pray for discernment, then trust that my Heavenly Father will protect me.

—Penney Schwab

*Thank You, Lord, for using a trampoline bed
to increase my trust in You.*

specks

Then you will see clearly to take the speck out of
your brother's eye. —Matthew 7:5 (ESV)

I hate getting anything in my eyes. The smallest speck can blur my vision and make me feel unbalanced and dizzy. The intrusion consumes my thoughts and actions until I remove the irritating item.

Every time I get something in my eye, I am reminded of the above verse in Matthew. I think of the logs in my life: pride, selfishness, disobedience. These sinful "irritants" consume me, keep me unbalanced and out of sync with God's plan. They prevent me from seeing anything or anyone else.

Jesus reminds me that I must first deal with my own specks and seek God's help in removing them. Just like the eyewash that removes the irritant in my eye, it is only through confession that God can wash away those spiritual specks so that I can see clearly to help others.

—Virginia Ruth

*May I learn to recognize and confess the specks in my eyes,
ask You to remove them, and in turn "see" to help
those around me. Amen.*

sanctification

. . . being confident of this, that he who began a good work in you will carry it on to completion until the day of Christ Jesus. —Philippians 1:6 (NIV)

I have to admit that the idea of sanctification—of being made holy—doesn't sound so hot to me. It sounds like dying to self, taking up my cross, and surrendering my defects. It sounds like very hard work.

Please understand, I'm not out robbing banks or the like, nor do I want to. But my own work in changing myself has been exhausting and not altogether successful. I am better, but not sanctified, apart from Christ. That's why I treasure this verse, because I understand Christ has already done the heavy lifting and will continue to.

The moment I accepted Christ, I took on His mantle of perfect holiness in God's eyes. The flesh and blood Isabella? Well, she's a work in progress. Thankfully, the Lord is at work in and through me and will be until the day I meet Him face to face.

—Isabella Campolattaro

Heavenly Father, may I rest in Your perfect holiness while You graciously work on mine.

impermanent

Heaven and earth shall disappear, but my words
stand sure forever. —Mark 13:31 (TLB)

Living in a tiny house with rowdy boys can be challenging
during the colder winter months. For Christmas one year,
I begged my husband to allow me to transform their tiny
bedroom into a fun zone of climbing and swinging. I had visions
of climbing walls, rigging ropes, monkey bars, and fabric swings.

At first he was less than enthusiastic about drilling holes into
the drywall, studs, and rafters. Then we remembered our plans
to grow our space in the future, which would involve demol-
ishing and renovating the boys' room. No need to protect an
impermanent structure.

Much like my husband's concern for damaging perfectly
good drywall, I believe sometimes I fiercely protect the things
in my life that seem safe, put together, and tidy. Perhaps remembering the impermanence of such things would free me to
say yes to the adventures God dreams up for me!

—Sarah Greek

*Lord, help me today to preserve my sense of adventure
over my fear of discomfort. Amen.*

ordered

We know that in everything God works for the good of those who love him. They are the people he called, because that was His plan. —Romans 8:28 (NCV)

I saw chaos and crises. My annuity check had decreased, my bank account was hacked into by someone in another state, my rent was due, and because it was the weekend, banks closed early.

I was driving down the street wondering what to do when suddenly the old saying "April showers bring May flowers" came to mind. Even though rainstorms can be disruptive, they also bring long-term benefits like fresh air, vibrant colors, and fragrant blossoms. The light bulb flipped on.

I asked my Heavenly Father, "Oh, so are You trying to tell me that after all these showers of chaos that I am experiencing today, You will bring about a sweet, fragrant aroma? One that will bring You glory and the opportunity for me to experience a fresh new perspective on how I see my circumstances?"

God's plan is ordered—even when things seem out of order.

—Teressa Robinson

Father, thank You for having all things ordered,
even when it seems out of order and chaotic.

glow

This little light of mine / I'm gonna let it shine.
— "This Little Light of Mine," Harry Dixon Loes

When a living organism produces and emits light, the phenomenon is known as bioluminescence. It's a fancy word for "glow." If you're lucky, you might witness it in marine life, from algae to crustaceans to many species of fish.

On dry land certain kinds of fungi present in decaying wood emit an eerie glow known as "foxfire." And who doesn't delight in the world's most wonderful example of bioluminescence—the firefly?

Human beings aren't bioluminescent, at least not scientifically speaking. But that needn't keep us from glowing. Unlike plants and animals, we don't glow to confuse predators or attract prey or lure potential mates. I like to think that people glow because our Heavenly Father put the light of love in our hearts, a light that lets us shine all over.

—Jennie Ivey

Keep me from hiding my light under a bushel,
Lord. Help me glow.

face-to-face

The LORD would speak to Moses face to face,
as one speaks to a friend. —Exodus 33:11 (NIV)

With modern technology, we can easily see the faces of loved ones or colleagues on a screen as we click Call or Accept to begin a conversation. Seeing the face of a person becomes more meaningful when there is an emotional connection with that person.

It is thought that the Hebrew word translated "face to face" in the verse above emphasizes the intimacy of the relationship, rather than implying that Moses saw the physical face of God. The intimacy implied is beyond vision; it's a sharing of deep friendship.

God could have made His communication known to Moses in other ways, but He found a way to be in Moses's presence and establish a relationship with His message. Much of my time is spent on planning how to befriend and help the world, and yet I continue to discover the simplest solution is the best—me just going or calling to offer and receive friendship, face-to-face.

—Connie McDaniel

Dear Lord, may I see the simplicity and yet power of taking time to interact face to face with others. Amen.

silent

The LORD is in his holy temple; let all the earth be
silent before him. —Habakkuk 2:20 (NIV)

I often pray about a word of the year, but in this particular year,
God seemed to be silent. *Maybe that's it*, I thought. *Maybe
silent is my word of the year.*

This felt like a stretch. My childhood report cards always reflected good grades, with a checkmark by the "talks too much"
box. Still, I craved more silent time in prayer and asked God
to speak to me through His Holy Spirit. As I meditated on the
word *silent*, not one, but *two* word combinations emerged from
the same set of letters.

Listen.

Lets in.

When I'm *silent*, I can *listen*, and that *lets in* God's voice.

I'd prayed for a word of the year and God gave me three.
He also gently checked the "talks too much" box and trained
my ear to hear His voice loudest.

—Laurie Davies

*Lord, help us to be silent before You and learn to hear
Your voice above all others. Amen.*

mirror

All of us who are Christians . . . reflect like mirrors
the glory of the Lord. —2 Corinthians 3:18 (PHILLIPS)

A large mirror hangs in the entryway of our house. I hung it there at the insistence of my wife, who explained that it would be helpful for checking my appearance before going anywhere. It's a great idea, and it works—in theory. Unfortunately, she and I often share conversations like this:

"Did you check the mirror before leaving?"

"No."

"Your hair is a mess in the back."

"I'm sorry."

Sigh. "You'll have to fix it when we get there."

Despite my spotty relationship with mirrors, the Bible says that, as a follower of Jesus, I reflect the glory of the Lord. I don't often see it, but I pray that others do. Today I hope to pray that single word—*mirror*—throughout my day to invite God to show His glory through me.

—Bob Hostetler

*Lord, please let my countenance and conduct
today reflect You. Amen.*

right

Be wise in the way you act toward outsiders; make the most of every opportunity. —Colossians 4:5 (NIV)

M y eight-year-old arrived home from soccer practice in tears. "Maisy was mean to me today," Olivia said. "She told me I kept making mistakes."

We sat at the kitchen table and unpacked what happened. "I kicked the ball and it hit her instead of going toward the goal," she explained. "And I told her that yeah, I did make a mistake, but I'm learning!"

I let her sniffle for a minute or so, then talked about their exchange. *How did it make you feel? Were her words helpful? What would you have said instead? What did you say to her?* I pointed out to Olivia that yes, Maisy was right. Olivia had made a mistake. But the way Maisy went about "helping" wasn't very helpful. Maisy had gotten so caught up in her need to be right that she hadn't thought about how hurtful her words were.

Today don't just work on being "right"—work on being kind.

—Ashley Kappel

Lord, help me remember that even when I am right, I need to lead and correct with kindness.

inspire

For our light and momentary troubles are achieving
for us an eternal glory that far outweighs them all.
—2 Corinthians 4:17 (NIV)

Troubles have hounded my little dog, Roman, all his seventeen years. A car ran him over at three, cancer took a toe at nine, and a cataract caused glaucoma that required removal of his left eye at twelve. A cataract in his right eye lets through only shadows. On top of it all, lifelong skin allergies cause frequent infections, mostly in his feet.

Yet Roman is full of joy. I took him for a walk on a sunny Friday afternoon in late winter, two days after a vet appointment for another foot infection. I caught him on video as he pranced down the street, turned to glance at me, and then skipped ahead with a burst of energy and delight. His love of life in spite of his troubles inspires me. The difficulties I face are truly light and momentary from heaven's perspective.

—Linda L. Kruschke

*Dear Lord, help me find joy in You and inspire
joy in others. In Jesus's name, amen.*

soap

If I then, your Lord and Teacher, have washed your feet, you also ought to wash one another's feet. —John 13:14 (ESV)

The scent of Ivory soap takes me back to thoughts of Mama and warm summer evenings. Living out in the country, we loved to run with bare feet all day. At bedtime Mama was insistent that she wash our feet.

My dear mother's love was that of a servant's heart. I'm sure she was tired at the end of her day. Her two newly adopted girls were gifts from God, and she treasured her time with us, even bedtime. We didn't realize it then, but she was teaching us how to love God, to make prayer time an important part of our lives, and to know that we could trust Him. Each night my little sister and I crawled into bed and had sweet dreams because of her act of love.

That memory of my mother's sacrificial love will be etched on my heart as long as I live.

—Linda H. Summerford

Heavenly Father, guide me daily to show Your love to my children and grandchildren so that my legacy to them will live through to the next generation.

nostalgia

Memory is the diary we all carry about with us. —Oscar Wilde

Y ou have to stop living in the past," an acquaintance said over lunch one day, months after my husband died. "You have to move on."

Before I could stop myself, I said, "No, I don't. My time with Keith was the happiest of my life. Why would I want to forget it?"

I still feel that way. My husband lives in my mind, and the nostalgia of those years draws me back and helps me smile at times when the tears of missing him threaten me. Nostalgia is the place where love dwells for me, protecting me from the pain of constant loss, welcoming me to the laughter we shared and the warmth of nestling together, that I could miss terribly if it weren't held safe for me. When something happens that brings me to a place of pain, I ask for nostalgia to wash it away and restore me to comfort and hope.

—Rhoda Blecker

I am very grateful to You for the strength of my memories, God of love, which have allowed me to build nostalgia into a source of nourishment that keeps me going.

keys

Take hold of my instructions; don't let them go. Guard them, for they are the key to life. —Proverbs 4:13 (NLT)

In my grandfather's job clearing repossessed houses, he found items the owners left behind. As children, we were most intrigued by the keys: odd-shaped skeleton keys, two-sided padlock keys, and tiny diary keys. We pretended they opened houses, cars, jewelry boxes, and treasure chests.

Unlike those keys, the ones I've found in God's Word open numerous treasures. Those are keys everyone wishes they had, and I can pray for God to lead me to them any time I need one.

- Wisdom: "If you need wisdom, ask our generous God, and he will give it to you" (James 1:5, NLT).
- Happiness: "The hopes of the godly result in happiness" (Proverbs 10:28, NLT).
- Health: "A peaceful heart leads to a healthy body" (Proverbs 14:30, NLT).
- Life: "The Son gives life" (John 5:21, NLT).

—Cathy Mayfield

Thank You, Jesus, for the keys to unlock the treasures found in Your Word.

neglect

Do not neglect your gift. —1 Timothy 4:14 (NIV)

I never expected to gain a mission statement from my seventy-something plumber. But that's exactly what happened.

When Jim showed up to fix my ceiling-high Victorian toilet, he brought along a rusted coffee can full of parts. "There she is!" he announced, fishing a shiny circle from a tangle of pre-owned parts. "Just what you need, Roberta. A brass ring." I joked that I'd been searching for the brass ring all my life!

When the job was done, Jim hardly charged me anything. As we talked a bit about retirement, he told me: "All I ever wanted was to do a little plumbing and make a few lives easier." After he left, those words stuck with me. Jim hadn't neglected the gift God had placed inside him. I wouldn't neglect mine either. I pulled out a notebook and started scribbling a story.

—Roberta Messner

Each one of us was put here to do something special, Lord. Help me not to neglect my gift.

amen

At this the whole assembly said, "Amen," and praised the Lᴀ᳀ᴀ. And the people did as they had promised.
—Nehemiah 5:13 (NIV)

I heard a sermon once that changed the way I view prayer. My church's pastor took the teal-carpeted stage with his usual kind smile and invited us to join him in Nehemiah. But the message that day wasn't part of a Nehemiah series; it wasn't focused on a chapter or a verse. The message was on one word: *amen*.

The word has a few different uses in Scripture, but what my pastor focused on was how the word was used to agree with something. It makes sense that after we pray, we say we agree with God's decision—but that's not where it stops. Because, my pastor told us as he leaned closer over the podium, in this passage *amen* means we agree so strongly we've decided to act on it.

Now when I pray, I'm not just kneeling by my bed or sitting motionless in a pew. I'm waiting expectantly for God to speak and preparing my heart for the *amen*.

—Haley V. Craft

Dear Lord, help me surrender my will to You so that when I say amen, I am willing to act on what You lead me to do. Amen.

words in this volume

Numbers listed refer to day number

authors in this volume

Numbers refer to the day number

a note from the editors

We hope you enjoyed *Pray a Word a Day* volume 2, published by Guideposts. For over 75 years, Guideposts, a nonprofit organization, has been driven by a vision of a world filled with hope. We aspire to be the voice of a trusted friend, a friend who makes you feel more hopeful and connected.

By making a purchase from Guideposts, you join our community in touching millions of lives, inspiring them to believe that all things are possible through faith, hope, and prayer. Your continued support allows us to provide uplifting resources to those in need. Whether through our communities, websites, apps, or publications, we inspire our audiences, bring them together, and comfort, uplift, entertain, and guide them. Visit us at guideposts.org to learn more.

We would love to hear from you. Write us at Guideposts, P.O. Box 5815, Harlan, Iowa 51593 or call us at (800) 932-2145. Did you love *Pray a Word a Day volume 2*? Leave a review for this product on guideposts.org/shop. Your feedback helps others in our community find relevant products.

Find inspiration, find faith, find Guideposts.
Shop our best sellers and favorites at
guideposts.org/shop
Or scan the QR code to go directly to our Shop

Made in the USA
Las Vegas, NV
18 October 2024

97078881R00213